A Museum to Instruct and Delight

A Museum to Instruct and Delight

William T. Brigham and the Founding of Bernice Pauahi Bishop Museum

ROGER G. ROSE

*Published in Commemoration of the
Ninetieth Anniversary
of
Bernice Pauahi Bishop Museum*

Bernice P. Bishop Museum Special Publication 68

BISHOP MUSEUM PRESS
HONOLULU, HAWAI'I

Library of Congress Catalog Card No. 80-69203
ISSN 0067-6179
ISBN 0-910240-28-0

CONTENTS

PREFACE

This 90th anniversary Special Publication is neither a history of the Bernice Pauahi Bishop Museum nor a biography of its first curator and director, William Tufts Brigham, though elements of both are to be found here. Rather, this is the story of the inception and birth of a museum, and its response to needs expressed locally for a functional museum of truly national character—in this case a museum devoted to Hawai'i and the Pacific, and developed through private means during that troubled period of the 1880's and 1890's when the Hawaiian nation itself faced the challenges of an uncertain and difficult future. Viewed from the comfortable perspective of 90 years, Bishop Museum's earliest days are not without parallel among similar institutions striving for expression in new and emerging nations of the Pacific today. This work, therefore, is dedicated to the spirit of a new and promising generation of Pacific museums, arising at last and in response to the needs and wishes of the peoples of the Pacific themselves.

I have many persons to thank for their roles in the appearance of this 90th anniversary Special Publication. First of all, I am indebted to my colleagues at Bishop Museum and elsewhere who have instilled in me a deep awareness and appreciation of the role of museums in the modern world. Specifically I wish to acknowledge an earlier contribution to Bishop Museum history, "The Bright Light of Knowledge," written in four parts for *The Conch Shell* by Brenda Bishop (1964-1965) to commemorate the Museum's 75th anniversary in 1964. Although the full story of the Museum's history has yet to be penned, the interested reader will find that brief account an overview that goes beyond the time frame of this present essay.

Among other individuals, I am indebted to Agnes Conrad and the staff of the Archives of Hawaii for making available numerous documents pertaining to the operation and management of the former Hawaiian National Museum. Its as yet little known history figured significantly in Bishop Museum's own founding and direction. I am also indebted to the librarians of the Hawaiian Historical Society and the Hawaiian Mission Children's Society for providing assistance during an earlier phase of this research.

To the staff of Bishop Museum I am most grateful for support and assistance through the years in making available documents under their care, especially Cynthia Timberlake, Librarian, and Anita Manning, Registrar. For access to and help with historic photographs from the Museum Photo Collection (all those illustrations reproduced in this volume), I am much indebted to Debra Sullivan. Likewise, Lynne Gilliland and Ben Patnoi gave generously of their time and talents in reproducing publishable photographs from old negatives and sometimes fading prints. I also wish to thank Patience Bacon for typing and Bonnie Clause for editorial suggestions on an earlier version of this manuscript.

Finally, this publication could not have appeared in a timely manner without the skills and dedication of the Bishop Museum Press editors, Genevieve Highland and Sadie Doyle. To them, and to others who have made helpful suggestions or otherwise provided assistance, I express my *aloha* and appreciation.

ROGER G. ROSE
CURATOR OF ETHNOLOGY

Honolulu, Hawai'i
September 3, 1979

ANTECEDENTS
THE HAWAIIAN NATIONAL MUSEUM

Little has been written of the role of William Tufts Brigham in carrying out Charles Reed Bishop's plan to memorialize his beloved wife, Princess Bernice Pauahi. While many factors helped nurture the idea as it took root in Honolulu during the 1880's, Dr. Charles McEwen Hyde is credited with the earliest suggestion for a museum of Hawaiian material. "Dr. Hyde's proposal was eagerly seconded by Honorable Sanford Ballard Dole," Brigham (1916b, p. 119), the Museum's first director, recounted a quarter-century after the Museum's opening "and Mr. Bishop was inclined to follow out a part of the suggestion." The founding of Bishop Museum is traditionally celebrated as December 19, 1889, the anniversary of Princess Pauahi's birth in 1831, but the date was selected arbitrarily and after the fact by early Museum trustees.

Although Dr. Hyde was instrumental in suggesting the Museum plan, many influences had been at work to help lay the necessary foundations. As early as the 1830's, the tradition of the natural history society had reached Hawai'i, where a few residents clearly understood the usefulness of preserving vestiges of the past. Thus, when the Reverend John Diell established the Seamen's Bethel in Honolulu in 1833, he fitted up a library and small museum in two rooms beneath the chapel, in the best New England fashion. Théodore-Adolphe Barrot (1978, p. 37) described this early effort while visiting aboard the French frigate *Bonite* late in 1836: "Adjoining the reading room is the cabinet of natural history, all the specimens of which are confined to some shells of the country and the coast of California, and to a dozen bows and arrows from the Fiji Islands." In November, 1837, the library and museum were formally incorporated into the Sandwich Islands Institute (see Schmitt, 1978, p. 100), which ship surgeon Richard Brinsley Hinds visited in June, 1839, during the voyage of the British warship *Sulphur*. By then, the display included "a few objects of natural history. These are not numerous, consisting of a few shells and minerals, a large black bear, a very few native weapons, poor [David] Douglas' snow shoes, etc."   1

(Kay, 1968, p. 128). Despite high hopes, the museum remained inconspicuous and eventually vanished without trace, black bear, snowshoes, and all.

As the Institute was struggling for recognition, a second museum came into existence in the 1840's in tandem with Punahou School (later Oʻahu College). Primarily a cabinet of curiosities for the edification of its students, the miscellaneous assortment of shells, minerals, fossils, ferns, ethnological specimens, and the like was given special quarters when the first permanent school building was erected in 1851. The "cabinet," with made-to-order sliding glass doors, occupied an entire wall of a downstairs room in Old School Hall, until the collection was moved to the new Bishop Hall of Science in 1885. Often neglected, and without anyone to assume responsibility for its growth and care, the collection gradually outlived its usefulness to the school and was dismantled piecemeal beginning in the 1890's (Alexander and Dodge, 1941).

While neither of these early attempts provided residents with a very clear notion of the scope or function of a public museum, the idea persisted until it finally bore fruit in the 1870's. After repeated urgings, such as in the essay "A Museum for Honolulu" in the May, 1856, issue of Abraham Fornander's *The Sandwich Islands' Monthly Magazine*, initiative was finally taken by the Legislature of 1872. On July 29 King Kamehameha V signed into law "An Act to Establish a National Museum of Archaeology, Literature, Botany, Geology, and Natural History of the Hawaiian Islands." The bill noted the Legislature's foresight and commitment to help to preserve the Kingdom's rapidly disappearing material heritage: "every succeeding year is rendering it more difficult to gather from the archives of the past the mementoes and relics of our early existence as a nation, as well as of the prehistoric age of these islands."[1]

Without ceremony, the Hawaiian National Museum opened in August, 1875, in one of the upstairs rooms of the newly completed government building, Aliʻiōlani Hale.[2] By terms of the bill of enactment, development of the Government Museum (as it was also called) was the responsibility of the Bureau of Public Instruction, which was granted $300 for the purpose. The task fell largely onto the shoulders of Charles Reed Bishop, new President of the Bureau's Board of Education. A native of Glens Falls, New York, Bishop had stopped in Honolulu in 1846 on his way to California, but decided to settle in the islands instead. The story of his marriage to Princess

Ali'iōlani Hale, completed in 1874 for government offices, faces 'Iolani Palace across King Street. The Hawaiian National Museum occupied one, later two rooms on the second floor right. Photographer unknown, circa 1882.

Bernice Pauahi in 1850 and their life together has been covered in the literature (see Kent, 1965).

Inexperienced in museum affairs, Bishop assigned the task of overseeing the fledgling Hawaiian National Museum in December, 1874, to Harvey Rexford Hitchcock, son of a prominent missionary family and incumbent Inspector General of Schools. Shortly after the museum opened, however, Hitchcock departed on a ten-month tour of American schools. He resigned his dual post shortly after returning to become principal of Lahainaluna Seminary. Hitchcock's successor, appointed curator in August, 1877, was David Dwight Baldwin, another missionary son, then teaching at Lahainaluna.

Despite a promising beginning, growth of the National Museum during the Board of Education's administration was as slow as it was uninspired. Not only was the nascent museum handicapped by lack of a resident curator during its critical period of establishment, but it also suffered from a lack of experienced personnel capable of expending, in any organized or meaningful fashion, its modest biennial appropriations, amounting to some $3,800 over the period 1872 to 1882. While Hitchcock's brief stint with the museum was commendable, Baldwin's five-year tenure as second curator proved lackluster at best. Neither man was able to generate public confidence in the developing institution.

3

Emma Metcalf Beckley Nākuina, Curatrix of the Hawaiian National Museum, 1882-1887. Photo from her booklet, *Hawaii: Its People, Their Legends,* 1904.

In the community, dissatisfaction with the National Museum gradually surfaced, culminating, in the spring of 1882, in a series of vitriolic newspaper attacks spearheaded by Walter Murray Gibson. It was perhaps no coincidence that Gibson, the controversial proponent of "Hawaiʻi for the Hawaiians," had found a convenient political tool in the National Museum. Achieving prominence during the government crisis of May, 1882, when King Kalākaua appointed him Premier and Minister of Foreign Affairs of the new regime, Gibson immediately wrested the National Museum from Bishop and the Board of Education and transferred it to his own control within the Department of Foreign Affairs. He persuaded the Legislature, then in session, to appropriate $3,000 for maintenance of the languishing museum during the 1882-1884 biennium and appointed as curator Emma Metcalf Beckley (later Nākuina), daughter of Theophilus Metcalf, a Harvard-educated engineer, and Chiefess Kāʻilikapuolono of Kūkaniloko.

For the next five years, Gibson and Beckley pursued the interests of the museum with enthusiasm as well as imagination, but a series of ill-conceived political maneuvers soon linked the institution too closely with impending disaster. In 1883, for example, a year after coming to power, Gibson launched the schooner *Julia* to Micronesia and Melanesia on a combined labor recruiting and pseudo-diplomatic mission aimed at establishing Hawaiian primacy in the Pacific. Unfortunately, the press responded by directing bitter personal attacks against Frederick Lee Clarke, the special agent Gibson had sent along to collect natural history and ethnological specimens, and the *Julia's* wreck and resultant scandal cast a pall over the museum. Even though the institution subsequently benefited through generous legislative support and other of Gibson's pet projects, the final embarrassment proved too much when the Premier dispatched another National Museum collector on the infamous *Kaimiloa* expedition to Samoa in 1886-1887. Gibson had hoped to strengthen the Polynesian ties between an independent Samoa and the Kingdom of Hawai'i, but instead the mission came perilously close to precipitating an international incident by upsetting the delicate balance of power being worked out there by Germany, Britain, and the United States.

On the whole, Gibson's fiscal policies and grandiose political schemes proved as devastating to the museum's image as to the Kingdom's fragile economy. On the heels of the Samoan fiasco, he was removed from office in the revolution of June 30, 1887, and expelled from the islands. When the Reform Government came to power armed with the "Bayonet Constitution," the economy-minded Special Session of the Legislature canceled all current and future appropriations, dismissed the curatrix (as Mrs. Beckley preferred to be called), and effectively brought further development of the National Museum to a grinding halt. Against this background, Bishop Museum came into existence.

Bernice P. Bishop Museum today

MRS. BISHOP'S HAWAIIANA COLLECTION

The immediate stimulus for establishing Bishop Museum was the passing of the three last high-ranking female *ali'i* of the Kamehameha dynasty—Ke'elikōlani, Pauahi, and Emma. Princess Ruta Ke'elikōlani, who died on May 24, 1883, was the half-sister of Kamehameha IV and Kamehameha V, and was said to be the wealthiest woman in the islands. Her extensive personal properties and lands, which she had inherited from Princess Victoria Kamāmalu and Governor Mataio Kekūanaō'a, were bequeathed to Bernice Pauahi Bishop, second cousin and closest surviving relative of Ke'elikōlani. Mrs. Bishop died less than a year and a half later, on October 16, 1884. Her combined land holdings, amounting to about one-ninth of the Kingdom, were set aside to form the Bernice Pauahi Bishop Estate, the proceeds of which were directed solely toward the founding and upkeep of The Kamehameha Schools, as provided by her will.

Mrs. Bishop bequeathed her personal property—including a valuable Hawaiian ethnographic collection—to her husband, who was destined to take a lifelong interest in its preservation.

7

Princess Ruta Ke'elikōlani, whose lands formed the nucleus of the Bernice P. Bishop Estate and foundation for The Kamehameha Schools, its sole beneficiary. Photo, M. Dickson, circa 1880.

Although Bishop apparently had not yet fixed upon the idea of an all-encompassing museum in her memory, through his experience with the Hawaiian National Museum he had no doubt realized the urgent need for preserving the cultural legacy of the past. That he had at least discussed a limited museum proposal with Mrs. Bishop is clear, however, for shortly after the opening of the museum bearing her name, Bishop wrote Brigham, its curator, regarding some family silver that he desired should "form a part of a museum of Hawaiian curios. Of course, Mrs. B. never anticipated quite such a Museum as we have made."[3] It is also probable that Dowager Queen Emma, widow of Kamehameha IV and one of Pauahi's last surviving relatives, had deliberated the fate of her own Hawaiian collection with the Bishops, but her death intervened before definite plans could be formulated.

Queen Emma's death on April 25, 1885, may have been the final impetus leading to Bishop Museum's founding. In failing health, the Dowager Queen prepared her will five days after Mrs.

Dowager Queen Emma, with silver baptismal vase presented by Queen Victoria for christening of her godson. Death of the four-year-old Prince of Hawai'i in 1862 left Emma and King Kamehameha IV heartbroken. Photo, A. Montano, circa 1880.

9

ernice Pauahi Bishop. "A bright light
nong her people, her usefulness survives her earthly
e"—Memorial inscription over Polynesian Hall entrance.
ioto, M. Dickson, circa 1875.

Bishop's passing, adding the following codicil on November 19, 1884, just before sailing to Hilo for a change of scene and hope of recovery:

> I give and bequeath to Charles R. Bishop, Esq., of Honolulu, Oahu, H. I., all my native curiosities, such as Kahilis, Calabashes, Feather capes and leis, and all and sundry the various articles belonging to me coming under the head of Hawaiian curiosities, together with the silver baptismal vase presented to me by H. M. Queen Victoria, Queen of England, on condition that at some future day they, together with all similar articles belonging to the late Bernice Pauahi Bishop, or to Charles R. Bishop, aforesaid, be presented by him to certain parties (hereafter to be named by him), as trustees of an institution to be called the Kamehameha Museum, such a museum to be under such rules and regulations as said Charles R. Bishop and the Trustees shall direct.[4]

Unfortunately, only her administrator, Alexander Joy Cartwright, had witnessed the codicil, and it was not legally binding. Nevertheless, when the *Daily Pacific Commercial Advertiser* published Emma's will under the headline "An Incomplete Codicil That Should Be Carried Out," the editor urged, in the first of several such statements, that it "should most certainly be given effect to, as the latest expression of her intention regarding the founding of an institution which should preserve the historical traditions and customs of the native Hawaiian race."[5]

During the next few months, Emma's wishes for the founding of a "Kamehameha Museum" remained a topic of public interest. Inadequacies of the Hawaiian National Museum, apparent to anyone who had visited it, also helped render the establishment of a worthwhile museum all the more imperative. By the end of the summer, the *Saturday Press* informed its readers of what appears to be Mr. Bishop's first public announcement regarding plans for a new museum: "We have learned with pleasure that a gentleman of proven liberality to education and science has under consideration a project to give to the public a worthy museum of Hawaiian antiquities. The nucleus of such a museum exists in three or four private collections in this city. It would be disastrous to any such attempt if the best of these collections were permitted to leave the country. It is to be hoped that none of them will be so permitted."[6]

Charles Reed Bishop, 1822-1915.
Carte d'visite, B. F. Howland & Co.,
San Francisco, 1866.

11

A month later, on September 5, 1885, the *Daily Honolulu Press* described Bishop's plans more fully:

A NATIONAL MUSEUM

We have it on good authority that Charles R. Bishop has in contemplation the establishment of a museum of Hawaiian antiquities. The relics, curios and industrial articles belonging to the estate of the late Mrs. Bishop form a valuable nucleus for such a museum. It was contemplated by Queen Dowager Emma to leave her relics and curios in trust to Mr. Bishop to be joined with those of Mrs. Bishop for the purpose first above mentioned. The unfortunate fact that the codicil of the late Queen's will, making such provision, was unsigned has delayed the immediate transfer of the relics in question, though it is earnestly to be hoped that they will eventually be devoted to the desired end. Dr. Arning has made during his two years residence, a very creditable collection, which he will sell at a fair price. One or two other private collections will be sold on equally favorable terms—for the above mentioned purpose.

If circumstances so aid Mr. Bishop that he is enabled to carry out his public-spirited project the nation will be greatly the gainer. "If done it is well that it be well done and done quickly" as the day is not distant at which a museum will be impossible.

Just over a year later the matter of the incomplete codicil was finally settled, clearing the way for Bishop to incorporate Queen Emma's collections into his proposed museum. At a meeting of the trustees of Queen's Hospital on September 15, 1886, the residuary legatees, Prince Albert Kūnuiākea and the Queen's Hospital, jointly consented on motion of Archibald S. Cleghorn to convey "to Charles R. Bishop and his successors and trustees the Hawaiian curiosities which belonged to the Dowager Queen and which she intended should be so conveyed as indicated in the Codicil of her Will signed November 19, 1884, it being understood that such curiosities are to be placed with other native curiosities which belonged to the late Bernice Pauahi Bishop and with others which may be added thereto, at an institution or museum for preservation."[7]

The next day *The Daily Herald* summarized the momentous agreement:

MUSEUM OF ANTIQUITIES

A special meeting of the Board of Trustees of the Queen's Hospital was held yesterday. It was called to consider the question of conveying the Hawaiian antiquities and curios, devised to the Trustees by the will of the late Queen Emma, to the Hon. C. R. Bishop for a projected public museum. Mr. Bishop had some time ago formed the purpose of founding a museum of Hawaiian antiquities, with the collection of his late consort, Princess Bernice Pauahi Bishop, as the nucleus. Prince Albert Kunuiakea, one of the devisees under the lamented Queen's will, had signified his willingness to transfer his portion of the collection to Mr. Bishop's custody, provided the Trustees would do the same with theirs. It was conceived by the Trustees of the Queen's Hospital that it would be a pity to sell the late Queen Dowager's fine collection, thus having it scattered and probably in large part sent out of the country, for the comparatively small amount that would thereby be realized for the Hospital. It is understood that Mr. Bishop contemplates the erection of a building for the Museum, which will be an ornament to the city, an attraction to visitors, and a conservatory of relics of ancient Hawaiian life, now disappearing fast. The project is one worthy of that gentleman. It is creditable to the public spirit of the Trustees of the Queen's Hospital, that they should so readily grant to the Museum the valuable collection bequeathed to them.[8]

With Bishop's resolve to found a museum of Hawaiian antiquities now a matter of public record, he had numerous decisions to make concerning its location, character, administration, and function. Although two years' delay was to intervene while plans for The Kamehameha Schools materialized, it is perhaps at this point that Hyde's contributions are most significant. Dr. Charles McEwen Hyde had come to Hawai'i in 1877 at the request of the American Board of Commissioners for Foreign Missions (ABCFM) to oversee development of the North Pacific Missionary Institute, a theological school for training Hawaiian reinforcements to the Micronesian missions. But his ambitions were by no means limited to this task alone, and he played a leading role in nearly

Rev. Charles McEwen Hyde, D.D. Plaster bas-relief
signed and dated by British sculptor Allen
Hutchinson, January 8, 1897. Bishop Museum Coll.
Photo, Ben Patnoi.

every significant educational and religious movement in Honolulu from the day of his arrival until his death in 1899 (Kent, 1973).

As a friend and adviser in the Bishop household, Hyde appeared a natural choice as trustee for the Bernice P. Bishop Estate. When Mrs. Bishop's will was probated on December 2, 1884, he was, in fact, her first choice after her husband.[9] Intimately concerned with the education and welfare of Hawaiian youth, Hyde was probably instrumental in the first place in counseling Mrs. Bishop on utilization of her great personal wealth. Authoring *The Prospectus of the Kamehameha Schools* late in 1885, he set forth the objects and methods of the institution as outlined in general terms in her will (Kent, 1973, pp. 168, 340-343). In short, Hyde became "the centering force in evolving the philosophy, principles of operation, and the program of studies of the new institution" (Kent, 1973, p. 165).

Hyde and the other trustees of the Bishop Estate were also delegated a second responsibility: to create an institution in keeping with the codicil of Queen Emma's will, which authorized Bishop to name certain parties "as trustees of an institution . . . to be under such rules and regulations as said Charles R. Bishop and the Trustees shall direct." To Bishop, a man of conservative principles, it seemed only natural that he should designate the same trustees to carry out both plans, which he considered to be related in scope and character.

Hyde's philosophy is also evident in the creation of Bishop Museum. Familiar with the museum concept as an educational tool, Hyde had once elaborated in some detail the notion of "a Biblical Museum to illustrate the manners and customs to which allusion is made in the Bible"

14

(Kent, 1973, p. 92). His beliefs were strongly supported by a friend and colleague, the Reverend William Brewster Oleson, principal of the Hilo Boys' Boarding School. A strong proponent of vocational education for Hawaiian youth, Oleson emphasized the pedagogical value of "curiosity cabinets" in a little-known essay entitled "Hawaiian Antiquities," which appeared in *The Friend's* educational column (of which he was editor) for February, 1886:

> It is quite inside the truth to say that Hawaiians of the present generation know by actual observation more about some of the startling inventions of recent years than about the tools and implements used by their immediate predecessors. It is not an uncommon occurrence to find large numbers of Hawaiian boys from fourteen to eighteen years of age who never have seen a Hawaiian spear or handled an ancient Hawaiian paddle. Quite as much actual information concerning Hawaiian antiquities could be gathered from a Beacon street boy playing on Boston Common within a stone's throw of Somerset street [that is, the ABCFM Museum], as from the average Hawaiian boy in our island schools. It is apparent to the most thoughtless that there are lost arts in Hawaiian national history. And it may be seriously asked whether there is not great likelihood that there will be a lost past likewise . . .
>
> It is well that the schools should emphasize the essential nobility of the privileges that civilization has conferred on Hawaiian youth. But to do this there must be an acquaintance with what was characteristic of the pagan past. The teacher should have at hand such accessories as can be found in almost any ordinary collection of Hawaiian antiquities. In the hands of private individuals here on the islands are numerous relics of the past that serve little better purpose than to occasionally satisfy the curiosity of English or American tourists. What a wise disposition could be made of the collections, not only by contributing them to Oahu College, but to the higher schools for Hawaiians on the various islands. Let the native boys and girls of today see with their own eyes what the past has bequeathed that they may intelligently realize how inestimable are the blessings of the present. What an invaluable possession would a collection of kapas, war implements, tools, and household utensils be to such schools . . . Who will be the first to found a cabinet . . .?

Oleson's essay might well have served as the initial prospectus for Bishop Museum, at least insofar as Bishop and the Estate trustees then envisioned the embryonic institution—an adjunct to

The Kamehameha Schools. At any rate, the trustees were in sufficient accord with Oleson's views to appoint him first principal of the new schools two months after the essay appeared.[10]

Transferring from Hilo to Honolulu early in the summer of 1886, Oleson, with Hyde and the other trustees, began to implement construction plans for The Kamehameha School for Boys. A site was selected on Bishop Estate land in Kalihi-Pālama, about two miles west of Honolulu (location of the present Bishop Museum complex). Roads were cleared and the lava-strewn lot was fenced with boulders removed from the grassy fields. One of Honolulu's early artesian wells was drilled by J. A. McCandless, promising sufficient water for the needs of the institution and the few houses in the neighborhood.[11] Principal Oleson's future home was staked out on a plateau near the center of the 85-acre lot, on a low hill commanding a panoramic view of the city, the Pacific Ocean, and the Koʻolau and Waiʻanae mountains.[12] Apparently the first building completed, it was ready for occupancy in January, 1887, when Oleson returned from a brief trip to San Francisco, bringing plans for additional buildings to be constructed during the next few months.[13] On October 3, 1887, classes finally began, and a month later the still unfinished premises were opened to public inspection. King Kalākaua, members of the royal family, delegates from the newly convened Special Legislature of 1887, and curious citizens gathered on November 4 to celebrate the opening.[14]

The Kamehameha School for Boys in operation at last, Bishop was freed to attend to practical matters relating to his museum. Sympathetic to Oleson's precepts stressing the value of Hawaiian antiquities as instructional materials for Hawaiian youth, Bishop felt that a site near the

16

The Kamehameha School for Boys about the time of opening in 1887. Two original dormitory buildings are still extant on Bishop Museum grounds. Photographer unknown.

school would therefore be most appropriate. This at least is the view Hyde expressed some years later in addressing a Founder's Day gathering at the museum, December 19, 1894:

> It was Mr. Bishop's desire, in locating the Museum on these premises, to perpetuate what of public interest, of national interest, of personal interest, there is in this extensive and unique collection of Hawaiian antiquities and relics. Heredity and environment are two potent factors in the development of races and individuals. It is Mr. Bishop's desire that these memorials of the past shall furnish suitable instruction and intensify patriotic enthusiasm in the Hawaiian youth of both sexes brought into these buildings, under these influences, for education and training, and, as such, they properly form a part of the equipment of these schools.[15]

The name finally adopted for the new institution (not "Kamehameha Museum," as proposed by Queen Emma and echoed for many months in the press) was recorded at the Bishop Estate trustee meeting held December 2, 1887: "Mr. Bishop stated that it was his intention to build a Museum on the school premises to be called 'The Bernice Pauahi Bishop Museum,' and asked consent of the Trustees to do this, and the privilege of using what material may be on the premises."[16] Granting permission, the trustees examined the building plans and also agreed to visit the grounds on January 3, 1888, to examine the site already staked out for the proposed structure, on the plateau a few hundred feet oceanward of Oleson's house.

Construction began in the spring of 1888. Troubled by vivid memories of the disastrous Chinatown fire of April 16, 1886, which devastated several square blocks and destroyed a million dollars worth of property, Bishop was eager to remove Mrs. Bishop's collections from the semi-basement of Keōua Hale, the wooden mansion on Emma Street that she had inherited from Princess Keʻelikōlani. In anticipation, he had plans drawn by William F. Smith of the San Francisco architectural firm of Smith and Freeman for a two-story stone structure of three rooms and entrance hall, in a derivative Romanesque style made popular in New England by Henry Richardson. The building was to be constructed of cut lava stone quarried mostly from a site on the grounds, under the supervision of William Mutch, stone mason and carpenter, and Robert

Lishman, contractor. The cost of the building, about $60,000, was ultimately provided entirely by Bishop.

An article on The Kamehameha Schools in the *Daily Bulletin* for May 22, 1888, gave the public its first hint of the new structure.

> Hon. C. R. Bishop will soon erect a building for the Kamehameha Museum, which will architecturally be a notable addition to the public buildings of Honolulu. It is designed to make it a complete repository of all matters pertaining to Hawaiian Archaeology.
>
> Queen Emma's collection of Hawaiian antiquities will be added to the large and varied assortment gathered by the late Mrs. Pauahi Bishop. Judge Fornander's collection of Hawaiian myths and legends will also be deposited in this museum.

A month later, a reporter for the *Daily Pacific Commercial Advertiser* visited the site in quest of a story on the school's first annual closing ceremonies. The article called attention to "Quarrymen in large numbers . . . operating on the dark basaltic rock deposits, getting out a superior quality of building stone both for the Memorial Hall to be erected on the campus and for the projected Bishop Museum of Hawaiian Antiquities."[17] Another reporter covering the June 22 closing exercises observed, "The foundations are laid, and several courses of stone already in place for the new Bishop Museum in a central position on the grounds. The stone is handsomely dressed from the rough clinker rocks that encumber the grounds. A large quarry near the eastern entrance is in full activity."[18]

During the following months, occasional visitors logged the progress of the new building as it grew slowly upward. In February, 1889, the school's monthly magazine, *Handicraft,* noted that "Work on the Museum is progressing nicely. It will be one of the finest native stone buildings ever erected." By June, when the premises were again opened for the school's second annual closing exercises, the building had reached the stage of roofing. "Its architectural design is now completely displayed," commented the *Daily Bulletin,* "showing it to be one of the noblest buildings of Honolulu. The stone was nearly all quarried and dressed on the grounds."[19] With sportsmanly pride, a writer for that same newspaper remembered in another column, "Where the stone was

Original Bishop Museum building shortly after completion, summer 1890. Bishop Hall, main administrative and classroom building for The Kamehameha Schools, is under construction at left. Both buildings were designed by William F. Smith of San Francisco and erected under the supervision of Robert Lishman, and William Mutch. Photo, W. T. Brigham.

being quarried for the Bishop Museum at the first anniversary of the Kamehameha Schools, is now a first-rate baseball ground on which the famous club of that institution trains."[19]

Toward the end of the year, while covering another Founder's Day celebration at the school on December 19, 1889, *The Friend* remarked, "The costly Museum, an elegant structure, is nearly ready for occupancy."[20] By April, 1890, some two years after construction had begun, interior work was at last reported to be "approaching completion."[21] The *Handicraft* for October that year urged, "It would be a pleasant feature of the observance of Founder's Day, Dec. 19, if the Museum were to be thrown open to public inspection on that day." Although the empty building may have been opened to informal tours, it was not until the following June that Bishop Museum was prepared to celebrate its first public opening.

The Kamehameha School grounds and Bishop Museum, December 28, 1891. Bishop Hall (foreground) was transferred to Museum use in 1961 several years after The Schools moved to Kapālama Heights (extreme right). Photo, W. T. Brigham.

WILLIAM TUFTS BRIGHAM, FIRST CURATOR AND DIRECTOR

Although Brigham once protested that he was "not responsible for the two rooms and picture gallery that constituted the Bishop Museum when he took charge of its care and arrangement,"[22] it is impossible to convey any understanding of the institution's development without substantial credit to its first curator and director. Without Brigham, the *Hale Hōʻikeʻike o Kamehameha*—as the Bishop Museum was sometimes known in the beginning—may well have become little more than a hollow shell housing a forlorn school cabinet of neglected curiosities. Breathing life and independence into Oleson's contemplated appendage to The Kamehameha Schools, Brigham rescued the Kamehameha relics from Bishop's incipient mortuary chapel and prevented the monument to Mrs. Bishop from lapsing into "a mere curiosity show, to amuse an idle hour . . . a mere Dime Museum."[23] Once accepting this new direction, Bishop himself did all that he could to aid Brigham in transforming Bishop Museum into "a permanent source of instruction, not only to this people, but to all others interested in Polynesian Ethnology and Natural History."[23]

Brigham possessed a rare combination of genius tempered with varying degrees of perception and bluntness, perseverance and bluster, that made him the right man for a difficult undertaking. "It was inevitable," wrote Bishop's biographer, H. W. Kent, "that he [Bishop] should turn to Brigham as he thought of establishing a museum. He was impressed with Brigham's whole scientific approach, his apparent practical and matter-of-fact personal qualities, and his unusual fund of general knowledge" (Kent, 1965, p. 186). Occasional bouts of ill temper and a quick pen aside, Brigham was, in short, well qualified to be curator, and later director, of the Kingdom's first workable museum.

Born in Boston on May 24, 1841, Brigham was a seventh-generation descendant of Thomas Brigham who had settled in nearby Cambridge about 1635. Through the years the well-connected Brigham family could claim many ancestors in the Tufts, Boutwell, Boylston, and other prominent New England families. His father, William Brigham, Senior, was a prominent Boston lawyer, as well as both a state and a United States Senator, amateur historian, and one of the founders of the

William T. Brigham on his first visit to Hawai'i, 1864-65. *Carte d'visite,* H. L. Chase.

Republican Party. Personally acquainted with many of the eminent men of the day, young Brigham, as had his father, attended Harvard College, graduating with the class of 1862 (W. I. T. Brigham, 1907, pp. 332 - 333). His M.A. in hand two years later, the budding young Curator of Mineralogy resigned his position at the Museum of the Boston Society of Natural History to make a fateful trip for "scientific observations and collections."[24]

Brigham first came to Hawai'i in 1864. Arriving via the bark *Smyrniote* on May 5 with a letter of credit to the Bank of Bishop and Co., he met Bishop that same day, and the two men inaugurated a friendship that was to last some 50 years. With Brigham was Horace Mann, a young botanist and son of the distinguished American educator. The two quickly set out to study the natural history of the islands; as Brigham wrote later, "it was at the suggestion of my Harvard instructors Asa Gray and Louis Agassiz (alas that their equals are not now on earth!), that I undertook the exploration of the botany and geology of the group . . . and this pursuit naturally took me all over. . . ."[25] Mann returned to Cambridge a year later with their collection of plants, minerals, corals, shells, and other marine creatures, while Brigham accepted an offer to teach for a term at O'ahu College.[26] During his island sojourn, Brigham visited frequently in the cosmopoli-

22

tan Bishop home, Haleakalā, where he came into contact with several individuals who would help him sustain an interest in Hawaiian affairs for the next 60 years.

In the fall of 1865 Brigham left Hawai'i by way of China and India, disappointed at having been unable to organize a scientific expedition into Micronesia and the Pacific. Gathering material instead for lectures on comparative religion and other subjects during the homeward trip around the world, Brigham delved into Hawaiian studies with immediate enthusiasm on returning to Boston nearly a year later. His *Notes on the Volcanoes of the Hawaiian Islands* appeared in 1868, stimulating a comparative geological work three years later, *Historical Notes on Earthquakes of New England, 1638-1869.* Also in 1868 Brigham published a translation from the French of Jules Remy's *Contributions of a Venerable Savage to the Ancient History of the Hawaiian Islands.* Five years later Charles Nordhoff reprinted the translation in *Northern California, Oregon, and the Sandwich Islands,* and sent an autographed copy of his book to Bishop, who had befriended Nordhoff while he was in Honolulu.[27] When Horace Mann died unexpectedly in November, 1868, Brigham stepped in to publish the botanical portion of their expedition, editing Mann's unfinished *Flora of the Hawaiian Islands* (1868-1871), and preparing several short papers on a number of new plants that the two of them had collected. Brigham also took over Mann's teaching duties as instructor of botany at Harvard in 1868-1869.[28]

The Brigham-Mann expedition of 1864 had marked the beginning of another friendship that was to last more than 60 years. Brigham first met Sanford Ballard Dole briefly while traveling in the islands, and the friendship blossomed when Dole stopped in Boston in the fall of 1866 on his way to Williams College. Dole spent part of his Christmas holidays that winter with the Brigham family, and young Brigham and Dole made plans in the spring to visit Philadelphia, Washington, Richmond, and other places. They were deeply impressed by the Smithsonian and Mt. Vernon, as well as other historic points of interest (Damon, 1957, pp. 55 - 57, *passim*).

Graduating from Williams that spring, Dole arranged by invitation of William Brigham, Senior, to study law in the Brigham law office. During the year that followed, Dole became practically a member of the family, met many influential persons, and greatly expanded his sheltered island background. Before leaving for Massachusetts, Dole had sent a box containing

Brigham's cabinet portrait, inscribed (reverse), "S. B. Dole Esq., with the aloha of Wm. T. Brigham, Feb. 1877." Photo, A. Marshall, Tremont Street, Boston.

some 21 crania from Kaua'i to the Peabody Museum at Harvard, where their eventual arrival endeared him to Director Jeffries Wyman and others in New England's tightly-knit scientific community. Pursuing mutual interests in natural history, Brigham and Dole spent as much time as could be spared at the Boston Society of Natural History, where Brigham now held positions as Curator of Geology and Botany.[29] Sharing his quarters in the Society's Library and Museum, Brigham encouraged his friend to take up the study of ornithology, an interest that Dole maintained for many years afterward. Despite a busy schedule, Brigham was admitted to the bar in September, 1867, and Dole finished his training the following year, returning to Honolulu in October, 1868, to practice law. The two met again briefly in 1873, when Dole returned to Maine to marry; Brigham was best man (Damon, 1957, p. 103, *passim*).

Fortunately for Brigham and his appetite for island news, Boston in those days was a kind of away-from-home center for Hawaiian affairs. The Hawaiian Club, organized by old island hands in January, 1866, served as a gathering place for visiting islanders, as well as a forum for promoting Hawaiian interests in the United States. Having taken an active role since returning from the islands, Brigham was called upon to edit the *Hawaiian Club Papers* in 1868 shortly before the death of the club's President, Captain James Hunnewell, an early Boston-Hawai'i trader.[30] Brigham contributed three papers to the 119-page volume: "Eruption of the Hawaiian Volcanoes," "The

Hawaiian Flora," and (with Hunnewell and Dole), "A Catalogue of Works Published at, or Relating to, the Hawaiian Islands."[31] He was elected president of the club in 1874, and during the next decade entertained many island visitors, including Mr. and Mrs. Bishop, whom he escorted to Harvard College during a tour of the city.[32]

From the day he left Hawai'i in 1865, Brigham harbored a lasting desire to return. Although a visit to the 1876 Centennial Exhibition in Philadelphia and reunions with old friends in the Hawaiian pavilion may have stimulated his concern, Brigham had always been deeply interested in Hawaiian culture and the changes confronting it. "It seems to me of the utmost importance to catch and preserve the meles and all legends relating to the former customs and religion of the people," he had once explained in a letter to Dole in 1874. "You and I can see that their extinction as a nation is fast coming, and the same is true of all the Polynesians; let then all that can be kept of their thoughts and actions. If I ever come to the Islands again I shall search out all the old heiaus and measure and map them and try to collect all possible accounts of the worship, of which we know little or nothing. Do urge all the earnest natives to bring in what they can."[33] Again he remarked to Dole while planning a trip to Mauna Loa in 1880, "I want to see and make plans of all the heiaus I can get to; see all the idols, and if I can do it get measurements and outlines of 100 typical Hawaiians from 14 to 90 yrs. old. No record exists of these measurements & important proportions."[34]

Brigham did return to Hawai'i that summer, stopping en route in San Francisco to see Mrs. Bishop for the last time, who was then visiting in the Severance home (Brigham, 1916a, p. 69). In Hawai'i, accompanied by a Boston friend, artist Charles Furneaux, Brigham hastened to the volcano to take photographs and make geological observations, while Furneaux sketched and painted lava flows and other volcanic phenomena.[35] The field work over, Furneaux remained in Hawai'i to become one of the islands' leading landscape and portrait painters. Brigham returned to Boston in the fall to analyze his materials, the results of which were incorporated into several publications, notably, *Kilauea in 1880* (1887), *Notes on an Ascent of Mauna Loa in 1880 . . .* (1888), and, years later, *The Volcanoes of Kilauea and Mauna Loa . . .* (1909).

No doubt this second trip whetted Brigham's desire to take up residence in Hawai'i—a move he had seriously contemplated but rejected because of ominous political conditions then brewing.

Brigham on muleback in Guatemala, 1883-86.
Photographer unknown.

The practice of law had never been very appealing to him, and on more than one occasion Brigham had sought other means of livelihood. In 1883 he joined a group of entrepreneurs in organizing The Tropical Products Company, a plantation on 5,000 acres of fertile land on Lake Izabel and Golfo Dolce, Guatemala (Brigham, 1887, pp. 338-339). During the next three years, Brigham made annual trips to Central America, but the company failed in 1886, forcing him to assign his estate to the family attorney, Alfred S. Hartwell—former Associate Justice of the Hawaiian Supreme Court (1868-1874) and one-time Attorney General (1876-1878). In the aftermath of bankruptcy proceedings, a shortage was discovered in a trust fund under Brigham's management, and he was arrested in February, 1887, for allegedly embezzling $17,000.[36] Although the charges were never proven, Brigham was forced to liquidate the remnants of his dwindling estate to make up the shortage. Scandalized, his family and friends cast him out, penniless and destitute.

Apart from financial and near social ruin, perhaps the hardest blow was the auction of Brigham's private library, which boasted many valuable first editions, including rare books printed in Hawai'i. Sadly, on April 5 and 6, 1887, some 1,397 lots of books and a miscellaneous assortment of minerals (many also from Hawai'i) were auctioned from the 101-page sales catalogue—Brigham's entire library of "Scientific, Archaeological, Fine Arts, Illustrated Anatomical and Classical Works."[37]

His major source of literary creativity suddenly dispersed, and with only dismal prospects of employment, Brigham began searching for ways to reorganize his life. Before the crisis, he had been negotiating with Senator Leland Stanford for the position of librarian at Stanford's proposed new university in California, but that possibility abruptly fell through. As a temporary means of support until something more permanent could be arranged, he set about organizing a series of traveling lectures. He also corresponded with Charles Furneaux in Hilo about returning to Hawai'i to write a history of the islands, similar to his most recent book, *Guatemala: The Land of the Quetzal, A Sketch,* published in 1887. Instead, Furneaux offered to lend his friend $400 to establish a law practice in Honolulu.[38]

Before any decisions could be made, however, Brigham was to have one more possibility to consider. The political storms brewing in Hawai'i, and the aftermath of the revolution of June 30, 1887, were about to intrude upon his personal turmoil and link the fate of the beleaguered Hawaiian National Museum with Bishop's plans for a monument to his late wife.

AMALGAMATION

Until 1888, when actual construction of Bishop Museum was just getting under way, the man who was to assume paramount responsibility in transforming Bishop's would-be cabinet of curiosities into a scientific institution of international significance was pursuing the idea of writing a history of Hawai'i. The book project, reminiscent of the Guatemala volume published a few months before, had been suggested to Bishop, who was skeptical. Unexpectedly, in the face of these uncertainties, Brigham was confronted with the prospect of taking charge of the new museum being planned.

In a rambling, hesitant letter dated February 27, 1888, Brigham responded to his old friend Dole's letters bearing news of the museum proposal, calling upon him to seek more information on the proffered curatorship and to intercede with Bishop on his behalf.

Your two letters of Feb 8th & 11th. came this morning. I have much rejoiced in your appointment to the supreme bench, as it is one of those things most eminently fit. I know you will decide as you think right even against a king. All your friends here are pleased, and send congratulations.

The book business is not so pleasant a matter, and I am rather surprised that Mr. Bishop does not take kindly to it: if he does not however, nothing more need be said, for it could not be published without some such assistance. The photographing on the Group will alone cost the sum I mentioned, and if done by me must be done soon, as I am an old man and not like a youngster who can wait. I ought to leave here in May at the latest, and take with me a trained assistant. Every thing but the pictures I can get better here than on the Islands.

What you say about the Museum interests me much, but it would be quite out of the question to combine the Curatorship with book-making. If I were appointed Curator the organization of the collections would demand all my time, and would mean a permanent settlement on the Islands. This I am not attracted to, in the present political state of the Kingdom. I am at present at work on lectures and articles for use another season, and must give all this up if I go to Honolulu, and again it would take a full quarter of the first year's salary to get out there. If I go into lecturing next Winter, I can easily make $3000 during the season of five months, and have the rest of the year for study and travel. I seem to be capable of lecturing and writing, is it wise to give up all that as I must if I leave the libraries and go to the Islands? . . .

My idea with the book is this: to leave here in May with a friend to assist me: take my photographic outfit, with a full supply of plates, and make suitable pictures of all the historical or interesting places on all the islands, even of the tops of Waialeale, [Mauna] Kea, [Mauna] Loa etc. Types of the people, plants, corals, fishes etc. Surf-bathing, spear-throwing, wrestling, in instantaneous pictures. My companion to assist in making such extracts from public records as I might need. Now as you well know travelling on the Islands requires a well-filled purse, and no poor man can do it. Neither would I undertake it without an assistant on whom I could depend. This I thought might take nine months or so, and then I should return to see the book through the press which is as hard work as writing it originally. Two volumes would be needed, and about 500 illustrations, which would cost, properly done, at least $6000, so the publishers would need a good sale to recoup. That is why they are unwilling to put out the preliminary expense. Now as to your suggestion about having [W. D.] Alexander supervise the work: that is out of the question, for while I shall be very glad to avail myself of all the information he will doubtless be willing to furnish, I don't propose to play second fiddle to any man. I should prefer either not to write the book, or to make a smaller one without going to the Islands at all. I want to make a book that will be a splendid piece of illustrative work containing all that any one here or in Europe would care to know about the Hawaiian Kingdom. I want portraits of the Missionaries, the Kings, the Chiefs: all that is known of the Natural History of the Group, including pictures of important indigenous species of birds, plants, fishes! I want pictures of kapa-beating, poi-pounding, hula-dancing, the Supreme Court, the Ministry. Such a book would be a more widely known memorial of Mrs. Bishop than any local building could possibly be.

Well if this cannot be, we must return to the other matter. Would it be proper to accept the Curatorship with the understanding that I might leave at the end of the year, for by that time the collections would be in order. I should then (supposing the term of service to begin in June or July), be able to return in time for another Winter's work in the lecture field. I should certainly like the work of arranging the Museum, but should not think of settling in a place, on such a salary, where there would be no chance of adding to it by outside work, like lecturing or magazine articles. It seems to me that all the real work will be done the first year. If I knew exactly when the appointment would be made I could speak with more certainty about accepting it, if offered, but I will put it this way:—if the book is not to be made—that is if Mr. Bishop declines to furnish the necessary funds, and the salary is to begin before next October, I will accept . . .

If Mr B. decides to have the book, I must go in the early Summer as my probable assistant is in college, and cannot be away after October. The dry season will be best for some of the journeyings and the photograph-taking. Then, again, if I am going I must have time to have the plates made and properly packed, and a few changes in my cameras made; while if I am not to be in the Islands next Winter, I want to know in time to make my appointments for lectures, which must be done early in the Summer, as they will be all over the country.

I think you understand my mind as well as I do myself: I want to go out in May (st[eame]r of June 1st.) and make the book. If I go out and take the curatorship I shall have more money in my pocket at the end of the year than if I had done the book: I might find something more profitable so that I could afford to settle permanently on the Islands, which I could not do on $2000. Do what you can to induce Mr B. to adopt the book but he must do it willingly: failing that I will drop the book and try the curatorship, if offered. I wish I knew something more about it, whether it is an independent position or under some beastly government officer (and I have known some of these to be pretty low, Gibson, for example). If the offer is to be made to me pray let me know as much as you can about what is expected, how the salary is to be paid, to whom I am responsible etc. I have sent by this mail, as you suggest, the copy of my [Guatemala ?] book (which I was keeping for you) to Mr B. and one to Furneaux at Hilo. . . .[39]

In due course, Brigham learned a few more details of the museum plan. The proposal, reiterated in a letter to Bishop some two years later, raised the possibility of amalgamation of the dormant Hawaiian National Museum and nascent Bishop Museum—and hopes of a new career for the despondent Brigham.

I had hoped that the original plan of the Government might have been carried out, which looked to the union of the Government Museum and your own, with my appointment as permanent Curator, to travel over the Group collecting not only antiquities but the flora and fauna as well, serving as historiographer and statistician as well. The original plan placed the appointment in the hands of trustees, free from political control, and the salary of $2500 to be paid by the Government. . . . The arrangement, study and care of such a collection as could be made here, would, I am sure, be a desirable and useful life-work. It would surely be worth to the Government and people, the small salary of the Curator. The mere investigation of the new blight, a thing wholly within my province, would be worth several years salary.[40]

Haleakalā, constructed about 1847 by Abner Pākī, Bernice Bishop's father, served as the Bishops' main Honolulu residence until 1884. Located near present-day King and Bishop Streets, it was once considered a possible location for Bishop Museum. Mr. Bishop is seated on the front porch. Photo, Ray Jerome Baker Coll.

Sanford B. Dole, later President of the Provisional Government and the Republic of Hawai'i, and first Governor of the Territory of Hawai'i. Photo, J. J. Williams, circa 1890.

Unfortunately, something interfered during the spring of 1888 to discourage merger of the government and Bishop collections, and the curatorship as originally proposed fell through. A quarter-century later, Brigham recalled a few more circumstances surrounding the original proposal:

> When the project took form in Mr. Bishop's mind for the erection of a memorial museum in the midst of the premises of the schools Bernice Pauahi had founded, Mr. Dole wrote to me (then living in Boston), noting the importance of having it a general museum of things Polynesian, and situated in the town, as there were then no easy means of getting to the rather out of the way schools. In reply I urged the former residence of the Bishops, built by Paki, Haleakala, on King Street, as a suitable site for such a museum, and suggested the inclusion of the existing Government Museum in the Judiciary Building [Ali'iōlani Hale], but Mr. Bishop was not then ready to adopt the more elaborate plan, and clung to the idea of a somewhat private and limited museum to preserve the combined Pauahi and Emma treasures . . . the whole to be in the care and custody of the teachers of the Kamehameha Schools (Brigham, 1916b, pp. 119 - 120).[41]

Although Brigham later recalled that "for some time there was considerable opposition on the part of the Government rather than on Mr. Bishop's part" (Brigham, 1916b, p. 121), evidence to the contrary suggests the Reform Cabinet did indeed support the idea of a combined museum, at least initially. When major portions of the Hawaiian National Library were transferred from its quarters in Aliʻiōlani Hale to the privately sponsored Honolulu Library and Reading Room Association early in 1888, for example, Minister of Foreign Affairs Jonathan Austin concluded rather pointedly in his departmental report to the Legislature that spring: "It is hoped that some equally beneficial arrangements may be carried out in relation to the articles in the Museum."[42] At the time, Bishop's intentions to develop a museum were already common knowledge, having been lauded on several occasions by the Honolulu press. The inference seemed obvious.

Moreover, the proposed merger of both collections with Brigham as curator had been discussed at a Reform Cabinet meeting held February 23, 1888. In attendance were Minister of Foreign Affairs Austin, Attorney General Clarence W. Ashford, Minister of Finance William L. Green, and Minister of the Interior Lorrin A. Thurston:

> Min For Affairs reported offer of J. Emerson to sell to the [Hawaiian National] Museum certain Idols & other relics of the Ancient Hawaiian times. Agreed that no purchase be made at present. Min Interior suggested a plan for the amalgamation of the Bishop Collection with that of the Government, involving the construction of a building for that purpose by Mr. Bishop, who now talks of building a Museum at the grounds of the Kamehameha Schools. In case of such amalgamation & the construction of a building in town, it is suggested that Mr. Brigham of Boston be engaged as Curator. Agreed that Min Interior should correspond with Mr. Bishop upon the subject.[43]

Unfortunately, if any dialogue occurred between Bishop and Minister Thurston, acknowledged head of the Cabinet, it resulted in a stalemate. Bishop had already staked out foundations for his new building and was proceeding with plans, even though actual construction had barely begun. As a matter of policy, the Reform Cabinet expected that any building housing the combined government and Bishop collections be centrally located, and thus more readily accessible than the somewhat isolated schools. Brigham's suggestion to convert Bishop's former King Street residence in the heart of the city was discouraged because of its wooden construction, and in any case, Bishop had already turned the building into a rooming house operated by a Mrs.

Dudoit.[44] The extant museum chambers in Aliʻiōlani Hale were also out of the question, partly because of the wooden interior, and partly because the space was far too small and already seriously overcrowded. Although Bishop perhaps could have relocated his building to another site, he chose not to do so. He still favored the limited idea of a "cabinet" to be associated with The Kamehameha Schools.

Brigham soon learned of the collapse of negotiations to amalgamate both museums, and with it his role as curator of the combined collections. The news came May 19, 1888, via another letter from Dole, which Brigham answered the same day:

> Your letter came this morning, and I confess that I was very much cast down. . . . I thought Stanford would give me a chance to make the library of his new university the best in the world, and for months that hope kept me alive. Then [Everette Edward] Hale thought a travelling tutorship would be the thing, and I spent much money in advertising. Then there was literary work to be done and I sent my circular to all the publishers. Then I hoped to write the history of the Hawaiian Islands; - that fell through. At last came the suggestion of the museum, and I was once more on the top wave: I saw work for me, and the means of living and paying the few hundred dollars I owe. The material I have been these many years collecting was not to be wasted after all. It is true that for the last two months life has been brighter for the planning how to build up a great museum in Honolulu which should be one to instruct, and delight. Here was something to live for, and I need not despair. Like everything else it has vanished into smoke, and has left very black ruins. . . . Did not that honored man [Alfred S.] Hartwell, after sacrificing my little property in his ignorance and laziness, seize for himself all the balance ($2500) and go to the Hawaiian Islands with the only fee he could collect in this city? What to him that his client was left penniless?
>
> James Austin says he will furnish me the means to go to the islands in search of something to do, but I am too old to go wandering about in foreign lands as a beggar, without anything definite. . . .[45]

Despite collapse of the museum proposal, Brigham continued with plans to come to Hawaiʻi anyway, hoping to resurrect the history project. Spending part of that summer with his younger brother, Charles, a San Francisco surgeon, Brigham wrote ahead informing Dole of his impending arrival, and made one further proposal:

> I wish the Gov't could be induced to appoint me historiographer of the Ids. for three years, to work up the History of Hawaii with photographs etc. As the political future of the group is soon to become interesting to Germany & England as well as to the U.S. it might be wise for private citizens (if the Govt. will not) to subscribe enough for the purpose. After the collapse of the native rule it will be less easy to do justice to the race & my sympathy with them would be of use. My brother wishes to find something for me here but I should prefer the Islands if possible to find employment there. . . .
> If the Govt could pay $1500 per annum & travelling expenses, I could do the work in good style. . . .[46]

Arriving September 18, 1888, Brigham lost no time taking steps to secure his future. Arranging to lecture at O'ahu College, he spoke on September 27 about Guatemala and "botanic wanderings" to a small gathering, including Chief Justice A. F. Judd, Bishop, and several other friends.[47] By then, however, owing partly to Dole's recommendations, Bishop had already reconsidered the history proposal and reached a decision regarding Brigham's future employment (see Kent, 1965, p. 187). Dole recorded the outcome in a letter to his brother George on September 25: "Brigham came by the *Australia* and is in good spirits; stays with us and goes on to the Colonies by the *Mariposa*. After returning from Melbourne he will stay for a year or so, working up his history of the Islands" (Damon, 1957, p. 208).

After two weeks in Honolulu, Brigham sailed on October 1 for Auckland, Wellington, Christchurch, and on to Australia and Melbourne's Centennial International Exhibition. From the *Mariposa* he wrote Bishop, who was now committed to the history—a work expected to honor not only his late wife but also his old friend from New York, William L. Lee, who had brought him to Hawai'i in 1846. Helping with the museum was of secondary importance, as Bishop's answer to Brigham on December 13 made clear:

> Your letter dated at sea Oct. 11/88 was duly rec'd.
> I expect to see you on your return, but as it is possible that I may be out of the way or

very busy while you are here, I will write you a few lines.

I would like to have you undertake the writing of a comprehensive, authentic and finished History of Hawaii and also to assist me with my museum, though how much there will be to do with the latter is quite uncertain now. You could at least assist me with advice about collecting and arrangement of interior of building and contents; and I might want you to help me actively in those matters.

My wish to see justice done to the memory of my friend (the first Chief Justice in this Kingdom) Wm. L. Lee is one inducement for helping about the history and as you are acquainted with my wife you will not omit to take due notice of her character and good works, and having acquaintance with the people and affairs of this country, together with the aid you could get from friends and acquaintances now living here, gives you advantages possessed by hardly any other person likely to undertake the writing of such a history.

Revd E^s Bond D.D. of Kohala, Mr. S. N. Castle, Gen^1 J[ames F. B.] Marshall, Edwd P. Bond (the last two of Boston) and a few others, are all that are left of those who knew Judge Lee personally and appreciated his services to this country. The records of the Privy Council, the Land Commission and of the Courts will show something of his work.

Of those who knew Mrs. Bishop in her youth, are her old teachers Mrs. H. Diamond [Dimond] and Mrs. Cook[e], and a few others who are old who are not likely to be spared many years more.

You will pardon me if I say to you that I think policy and success would require that you should keep clear of partisan politics and that you should endeavour to be on such terms with the King and people (native and foreign) as would give you access to all sources of information and all shades of opinion. If the King or others in authority should have reason to think of you unfriendly to or prejudiced against them, they would place obstacles in your way, and condemn your work in advance. Whereas did they believe you to be friendly or impartial they might help you to even more than you would want or would use.

It would be better also that it should not be known that I was assisting.

I do not feel like pledging to you four thousand dollars per annum for two years, but I will promise $3000 for one year and at same rate for any part of another year that your work may require with the understanding that during the whole time you will give me such advice and assistance about my museum as you can without interfering too much with your history work. And should I be satisfied that the sum promised is inadequate, I think I shall, after the first year be willing to do what may appear to be right in the premises.[48]

Leaving the Colonies, Brigham met and hired his assistant for the history project, a young man named Acland Wansey from Quirindi, New South Wales. He was a fellow passenger aboard the *Zealandia* bound for San Francisco. Arriving there two days before Christmas, Wansey "studied photography with a photographer," and the pair "set to work to get things ready for our return to the Islands."[49] Back in Honolulu, via the *Alameda* on February 18, 1889, Brigham applied at once for letters of denization, stating that he "was about to resume his residence for the purpose of writing a history of the Country."[50] The papers were delivered twelve days later by Secretary Mist of the Foreign Office, conferring on Brigham the privilege of permanent resident of the Kingdom.[51]

Settling temporarily with the Dole family, Brigham and Wansey began to gather material for the history. Within a month, Brigham had obtained from Minister of Foreign Affairs J. Austin a working library of some 101 titles, mainly reports and statistics issued by various government departments.[52] Six weeks later, he asked Minister Austin to help acquire from the British Admiralty a copy of the journal written by John Ledyard, a marine on the *Resolution* during Cook's voyage to Hawai'i. W. Horace Wright, a Foreign Office clerk (later to become involved with the Hawaiian National Museum transfer) forwarded the request to London with the comment, "There are persons here ready to meet any expense of such a copy."[53]

37

Brigham (center) and crew at Nāpō'opo'o, Hawai'i, surveying and photographing archaeological sites, circa 1890. Photographer unknown.

A few months after arriving, Brigham and Wansey established headquarters in a rented house next door to Dole, and there built "a fine dark room."[54] Some 30 years later Wansey recalled,

> As soon as we were comfortably settled we started off on explorations of the different islands, we photographed a number of heiau, natives at games, mat making, stone implement-making, etc., collections of kapa beating implements, stone implements, wooden bowls, mats, feather capes, fishhooks and lines and every thing that was of interest.
>
> When we returned to Honolulu our time was taken up developing the photographs, making notes of the various trips and arranging specimens of various things collected on the trip.
>
> A great deal of time was taken up reading every book and article that related to the Hawaiian Islands. Many books were loaned from abroad, others from people in the islands. . .[54]

The history under way, and construction of the museum building moving forward, Bishop, meanwhile, was quietly engaged in acquiring specimens for it. Originally, it was to have contained mainly the Kamehameha relics from Princess Pauahi and Queen Emma, plus a few objects inherited from Princess Keʻelikōlani and other aliʻi. Then, and perhaps at Hyde's urgings (see Kent, 1973, p. 93), Bishop purchased the first significant foreign collection for the embryonic museum on August 23, 1886—two dozen Micronesian curios from Joseph Swift Emerson, a local collector and government surveyor who had acquired most of them the previous May from Captain Bray and First Mate Carl Freywald of the *Morning Star,* the Micronesian mission ship.[55]

About this time, Bishop commenced negotiations with the American Board of Commissioners for Foreign Missions in Boston to purchase their museum's valuable collection of Hawaiian and Pacific antiquities. The committee reviewing Bishop's request was unsympathetic, recommending to the governing Prudential Committee on March 22, 1887, "that the Board do not sell but should loan to Mr. Bishop these articles, to be deposited in his Museum at the Sandwich Islands, until such time as the Prudential Committee shall ask for their return. After discussion the report was recommitted for further consideration" (Kent, 1965, pp. 215-216). Bishop's next attempt in the summer of 1889 to have the collection loaned indefinitely was likewise denied, as was a third

Keōua Hale, completed late in 1882 for Princess Keʻelikōlani at 21 Emma Street, was bequeathed to Mrs. Bishop the following year. It became Mr. Bishop's home in 1884, where he lived until moving to San Francisco ten years later. Photographer unknown.

request two years later. Not until 1895, and then through the intercession of both Hyde (the Hawaiian Board's Corresponding Secretary to the ABCFM) and Gorham D. Gilman of Boston, was the loan request finally granted. (Ultimately, the collection was purchased outright for $8,000 in 1896, the ABCFM having fallen upon hard times.)[56]

While negotiations with the ABCFM inched forward, Bishop continued to add to his collection by other means. His primary source was J. S. Emerson, who had accumulated in excess of 1,000 objects from Hawai'i and the Pacific by the end of 1887. When the government, at the Cabinet meeting of February 23, 1888, declined to purchase his Hawaiian materials for the expiring National Museum, Emerson sold the bulk to Bishop a year later. On February 16 and 23, 1889, two lots, by now totaling some 1,600 ethnological specimens—one of the Museum's most important collections ever—were delivered to Bishop's Emma Street basement, there to await completion of the museum building and a curator to take charge.[57]

A few months later Bishop acquired another local collection of note from George H. Dole, Sanford's older brother. This was a mixed accumulation of adzes, sling stones, polishing stones, *poi* pounders, mortars and pestles, lamps, sinkers, and so forth. Most of the objects had been unearthed by plow from sugar plantations on Kaua'i. As early as 1875 Dole had loaned 15 of the adzes to the Hawaiian National Museum for its opening, later withdrawing all but two on May 27, 1889, while preparing to move his family to Riverside, California. In financial straits, Dole sold the collection on September 28 through Honolulu auctioneer James Morgan. Bishop purchased most of the lot, expending some $356 of the total receipts of about $400.[58]

Thus, by 1889, Bishop was slowly beginning to accumulate collections for the as yet unfinished building. Enmeshed in his history project, Brigham, however, professed little interest in this "mere school cabinet of curiosities," which he dismissed as "simply a mortuary chapel, as it were, of relics" (Brigham, 1916a, p. 70). Even so, he could hardly have failed to notice the nearly complete museum superstructure dominating the horizon while attending Kamehameha Schools' closing day exercises that June, and Founder's Day celebrations six months later. Nevertheless, as he had intimated in their agreement of the year before, Bishop now sought Brigham's help with the growing collections. Brigham recounted later,

Kāhili from the collection of Mrs. Bishop and Queen Emma, on the grounds of Keōua Hale. Photo, W. T. Brigham, 1889-90.

Bishop Museum about 1892, consisting of Kāhili Room (left), Entrance Hall and Tower (center), and Hawaiian Vestibule (right), with Picture Gallery above. Photo attributed to W. T. Brigham.

When I transferred my residence to these islands . . . I thought very little of the school cabinet plan . . . I do not remember visiting the school grounds until the Museum building (the first of *cut* stone on the island), had been erected, when one afternoon Mr. Bishop came to my house on School Street and asked me to drive out with him and see what had been done. It was my first view of a building in which I took little interest, for I knew what school cabinets of curiosities almost invariably became in untrained and uninterested hands, and the appearance of the bare walls and unfloored interior was not in the least attractive to me, and I did not visit it again until Mr. Bishop showed me the Emerson collections and some other rather unimportant material that he had partly displayed in the basement of his house on Emma Street, and asked me to arrange these in the new building which had by that time been floored, and the kahili cases built into the smaller of the two exhibition rooms. . . .

I had already photographed the kahilis *en masse* in the garden of the Emma Street house, and also groups of other Hawaiian antiquities in the collection, for illustration in my proposed history, and I of course went out to Kalihi to see how it would be possible to arrange the specimens in the two very moderate sized rooms at my disposal before agreeing to Mr. Bishop's proposal: it was a rather uninteresting interruption to my historical studies, and besides, except for the cases in the Kahili Room, there were neither cases nor shelves, nor even tables for the exhibition or even storage of the very miscellaneous collection. The interior walls were all white plaster, and the koa stairway, very ugly architecturally, looked too bright against the plaster walls (Brigham, 1916b, pp. 120-121).

Entrance Hall and main staircase of native *koa* wood, before construction of doorway to Polynesian Hall at top of first landing. Hawaiian wooden image (right) from Trustees of O'ahu College; Maori carved house front (left) purchased from Eric Craig, Auckland. Photo attributed to W. T. Brigham, circa 1892.

Besides the history, one of the obstacles preventing Brigham from committing himself to the museum was the financial burden under which he was then laboring. He owed money, and the expenses of traveling and gathering data for the book were proving to be greater than the limited means his employer had provided. He was clearly troubled about his future when he wrote to Bishop on his birthday, May 24, 1890.

> When I came here I had been through a severe financial experience and from comparative affluence had been reduced to poverty. I had given up everything and had to borrow the means to come here. I have during the year been troubled with those anxieties which arise from insufficient means to pay one's debts, and which are fatal to the best literary activity . . . I am today 49 years old, and the prospect is not cheering—with $1,000 due and only the prospect of a temporary employment! . . . I want to live here permanently, if I can see my way to a simple living:—I have got to that age when the making of money does not seem the only aim of life.[59]

Still disappointed that the original plan to make him curator of the combined government and Bishop collections had not met with favor, Brigham continued to press for its revival. When Thurston's Reform Cabinet was replaced on June 17, 1890, following a particularly acrimonious feud that spring, Brigham may have sensed that the new administration might be inclined to go along with more of the old plan. (By that time the government had finally decided to lend its collection to the new museum.) Just before embarking on a five-week trip to observe the volcano,[60] he made one last appeal, in a masterful letter to Bishop dated July 6, 1890:

A remark that I casually heard yesterday leads me to write this note, as I leave on the Kinau early tomorrow, and shall not have time to say what I now write. You have all the material for one of the unique museums of the world, one which with comparatively little further outlay can be the Polynesian collection of the present advanced system of scientific exhibits, or on the other hand, and by inevitable neglect gradually disappear, as the once interesting cabinet of Oahu College has gone.

Surely you have laid out too much money for a mere Dime Museum: you have collected too many priceless things. Will you not go a little further and make it a permanent source of instruction, not only to this people, but to all others interested in Polynesian Ethnology, and Natural History?

I will come directly to my business in this matter, and then give some of my reasons for the proposition I make. I suggest that you appoint me Curator of the Museum for two years from Feb. 17, 1891, with a salary of $2,500 per annum, and put the entire arrangement of the collection in my charge. This seems to me the least time in which the Museum can be made tolerably complete. I should propose to have in connection with this work a class or classes in Botany composed of the most promising students of the Kamehameha School, and such of the public as might desire to attend, latter to pay me a suitable fee; these classes twice a week. In this way [I] should expect to train collectors who would complete the Herbarium without further purchase of specimens. The Shells, corals and fishes to be collected in the same way. All the plants now in your collection should be examined, identified, and remounted on suitable paper. The shells and corals to be prepared and named. The birds rearranged, and put in order. The names attached to the specimens. The ethnological specimens to be cleaned, repaired, where necessary, and arranged in ethnological sequence. Duplicates to be exchanged for desirable specimens, and all deficiencies to be filled where practicable. The labeling is a matter of no little importance; those affixed by Mr. Emerson being in very bad taste. A book should be kept in which every specimen should be entered, with its history so far as known, and its place in the collection. Photographs of the old chiefs should be collected and placed in the gallery; also

44

photographs of the idols and other Hawaiian relics, not now attainable. To this collection might be added views of the heiaus, etc. still extant. My belief is that if the Government and people saw in the two years how useful the Museum had become, they would make the office a permanent one, and thus insure the growth and permanency of the collection. Here the stranger, even if not of scientific tastes, can see the principal natural productions of this Group, and the resident can learn the name and nature of specimens not hitherto known to him. I think that every plant, every shell, every coral, every form of lava, every bird, insect and fish of Hawaii Nei should have a place in addition to the implements and fabrications of the natives. The connections of the Hawaiians with cognate races should be clearly shown in the arrangement of specimens of handicraft.

I hope to have the principal work of the History done by next February, but the Museum work would not interfere with that, the finishing touches would be done in the evenings. I naturally wish to be settled permanently here . . . If I have nothing to look forward to here after the History is finished, I must be looking even now for employment in the U.S. or the Colonies.

I have thus fully unfolded my plans and wishes, and have offered my services for the Museum; that they may be accepted, and my stay on these Islands thus be prolonged, I heartily wish, for the collections are worthy of care and study, and should not be treated as mere curiosities. My experience in the Museum of the Boston Society of Natural History and elsewhere has perhaps fitted me for the work . . .[61]

It may be said that the museum as a comprehensive, scientific, and educational institution stems from Brigham's proposal—and from Bishop's answer on August 18, 1890:

. . . the fact that, to carry out your suggestions for Curatorship etc., would add more to the expenses of the Museum than I had contemplated, is one reason why I had hesitated about adopting them.

The building for the Museum is a part of the Kamehameha School premises, and with what is intended to be put into it, is virtually the property of the estate, and under the control of the same trustees as the school is, but as I have paid the cost of nearly everything constituting or connected with the Museum so far, and intend to continue to pay for all additions—except such as may be loaned or contributed, I shall, no doubt really control so long as I may wish to do so . . .

I have concluded to give you that appointment with the understanding that, for the salary named you will devote your time and effort to making the museum what you have suggested that it should be, and can be, so far as the means furnished will admit of, and will not allow any other work to interfere with that object.

I shall have no objection to your teaching a class in botany on the school premises, but can make no engagement or promises in regard to it.

Your salary will be payable at the end of each quarter.

It is expected that the museum will include all that belongs to the Government collection, as a loan.

My claim to a part of your time for the current year ending Febr'y 17th, 1891, will no doubt be more availed of than it has been, since the building is now so far completed that some things in my house can soon be removed; and in fitting up cases, shelves etc. I shall require your advice and assistance from time to time . . .[62]

Brigham now had two jobs to confront. Until the new terms of employment became effective February 17, 1891 (the second anniversary of his moving to the islands), Brigham continued to work on the history, albeit with steadily decreasing enthusiasm. Instead, planning anew—and at last—for "a museum to instruct, and delight" began to demand more and more time, and the history was gradually pushed aside. Meanwhile, his museum in capable hands, Bishop sailed for San Francisco on November 21, 1890, and a long European vacation for reasons of health, not to return until December 10 of the following year.

THE TRANSFER

When the Legislature of 1890 assembled on May 21, Minister of Foreign Affairs Jonathan Austin summarized in his biennial departmental report the conditions under which the Hawaiian National Museum was about to be dissolved:

46

Early pastel post card of original Museum building and Bishop Hall (left). Published by Wall, Nichols & Co., Ltd., Honolulu, circa 1894. Photographer unknown.

Arrangements have been made with the Hon. C. R. Bishop for the transfer of the articles in the Government Museum to the "Bernice P. Bishop" museum [*sic*] as a loan under an agreement that they be returned to the Government on demand of His Majesty's Cabinet. A fine stone building is being erected for the accommodation of the Museum, which will include the valuable and constantly increasing collection of Hawaiian and other Polynesian curiosities and antiquities now belonging to Mr. Bishop, and which he will donate to the Museum. The collection received from the estate of the late Dowager Queen Emma Kaleleonalani will also be placed there. It is believed that those collections will be enhanced in value and interest to scientists and the public, by adding to them the articles belonging to the Government, and the effect of the combination of so many interesting articles for exhibition in a large, well arranged and safe building, will prove more attractive and valuable to our citizens, and contribute more to the pleasure and information of our visitors than the separate display of the collections under less favorable auspices. The building is in a forward state of construction, and will be ready for occupation within a few months from the present time.[63]

Austin's ministerial report is the only known document stating arrangements finally reached between Bishop and the Hawaiian government. No formal agreement has come to light, nor is it known precisely when both parties reached mutual accord. Minister Austin's report, dated March 31, 1890, marked the end of the government's current fiscal biennium, and the impending changes were publicized by the *Daily Bulletin* on April 29, 1890: "The contents of the Government Museum are to be transferred to the Bishop Museum at Kamehameha Schools. It is considered advisable that the Government collection, the Queen Emma collection, and the Bishop collection should thus be combined in one grand National Museum of Hawaiian and Polynesian curiosities and relics."

While timing cannot be established with certainty, several factors were at work to encourage rapprochement between Bishop and the government during the closing months of the 1888-1890 biennium. For one thing, a visit of inspection to the National Museum undertaken by Bishop, Brigham, and Wansey may have led to renewed discussions with government officials about the fate of the increasingly problematical collection. "About the latter part of 1889," Wansey recalled more than 30 years later, "We all went down to the Judiciary Building and examined the room up stairs, it was found too small and unsuitable and might easily be entered by thieves. Then it was proposed to build a museum where the old [Bishop] house was . . . Mr. Bishop seriously thought of building there."[64] By then, of course, construction at the Kalihi site was far too advanced to give serious consideration to relocation. Such a move no longer seemed necessary, anyway, since inauguration and rapid expansion of tram service after 1888 (Martin and Ramsay, 1960, p. 6) had already mollified the government's earlier objections to this decentralized location.

A more pressing factor had to do with conditions in Ali'iōlani Hale itself. Since the Reform Government had determined in 1887 to discontinue support of the National Museum, responsibility for its collections had become somewhat of a thorn in the flesh. Lacking a curator, government employees in the building often found it necessary to interrupt work to look after more and more tourists seeking entrance to the museum. Incidents such as the one reported by the *Daily Bulletin* on October 4, 1889, must have posed a serious annoyance to daily routine, prompting many to wish that the museum and its attendant problems be banished entirely from the building: "During the past few days no less than forty-three men from the Japanese warships, four merchants and four journalists of the same nationality have visited the Government Museum in Aliiolani Hale. This is exclusive of a large party of Japanese naval sailors who called during our reporter's visit to the Foreign Office this afternoon."

Yet another factor, which Brigham turned to advantage, was the rapid growth of the Law Library during the late 1880's. In December, 1885, it had been detached from the Government Library and moved into separate quarters in Ali'iōlani Hale under the Attorney General's care. A new source of revenue opened up when the Legislature of 1888 passed a measure to channel license fees from court practitioners to the Law Library. "It is estimated," one newspaper commented at the time, "that the new system will produce to the Government over $2000 for the biennial period, and this in addition to the regular appropriation will make quite a handsome sum to be expended on law books."[65] Housing some 3,300 volumes by February, 1889, the library soon outstripped the limited space assigned to it, especially once Chief Justice A. F. Judd announced his intention to make the Law Library "one of the best stocked" and "a credit to the country."[66]

When the Attorney General began to look around for his department's growing needs, the perfect solution seemed to lie in the quarters partially vacated by the old Government Library in 1888, and the adjoining room occupied by the problematical National Museum. As Brigham candidly explained years later, "a chance remark of the Attorney-General, that he needed more room and that the visitors to the Museum disturbed his department, gave me the hint and I urged him to use all his great influence to secure the transfer of the collections to the new Kalihi building and thus putting at the disposal of the law department the needed adjoining room. I was successful . . ." (Brigham, 1916b, pp. 121-122).

With formal arrangements worked out at last, the task of transferring the government collection awaited only completion of the new museum building. In anticipation, Brigham made at least two visits to the National Museum—August 19 and October 29—and in January, 1891, began preparing the collection for transfer.[67] William Horace Wright, a Foreign Office clerk (who had replaced Captain H. W. Mist two or three months before) was assigned to help.[68] A week before the scheduled transfer, the *Daily Bulletin* for January 23 observed: "Mr. H. W. [*sic*] Wright of the Foreign Office is taking an inventory of the articles in the Government Museum, preparatory to having them transferred to the Bishop Museum at Kamehameha Schools. Prof. W. T. Brigham, curator of the Bishop Museum, is checking the articles off for that institution."

Unfortunately, the death of King Kalākaua on January 20 at the Palace Hotel in San Francisco upset the orderly procedure. The King had gone to California in November for reasons of health, and the excitement generated on January 29 by realization of his death suddenly interrupted work in the National Museum. Brigham's reminiscences of that day recall the urgency with which events unfolded:

> [I] was superintending the packing of the specimens for removal when Captain Mist, [former] secretary in the Foreign Office, came hurriedly in and told me that the 'Charleston' was signalled with her flag at half-mast, and as Kalakaua was returning on her it was probable that he was dead. I at once went out and got all the help I could, engaged all the express carts to bring me packing cases, and before the end of that eventful day the whole collection was dumped on the floors of the new museum. A change of government might

keep the museum in its old place for the present, and I would take no chances (Brigham, 1916b, p. 121).

Amidst the confusion, Brigham somehow found time to rush to Dole's house early in the morning to inform him of the news, spend part of the afternoon aboard the *Charleston,* and later to escort Mrs. Dole and her cousin to view the cortege bearing the King's body to ʻIolani Palace (Damon, 1957, pp. 227-228)—all while supervising the hasty transfer of the contents of the National Museum!

A few days after the government collection reached Bishop Museum—very possibly the first specimens to arrive—Brigham reported to Bishop, still in San Francisco on the first leg of his 13-month vacation to the Carlsbad. Bishop's response brought up a problem concerning certain National Museum specimens temporarily out of the Kingdom. "Yes, I am glad that the Govt. Collection—the valuable part—has been recd. and that you are soon to begin to transfer the things at the house," Bishop answered on February 17 (the very day Brigham assumed formal curatorial duties). "You know that some things belonging to the Govt. Collection went to Paris and then to the Bremen Exposition, and have not yet returned. One very rare and choice thing—the [Kaumualiʻi feather] helmet, which I am very desirous of having. It was wrong to permit such things to go away, such as cannot be replaced."[69] Some months later, the articles that had been exhibited at the Paris *Exposition Universelle* of 1889 and the Bremen Colonial Exhibition of 1890 returned, and in November they were turned over to Brigham for Bishop Museum.[70]

Delving into his new duties as curator, Brigham devoted the next several months to moving, unpacking, and arranging specimens for exhibition. Along with the government collection, artifacts soon began to appear from the Bishop home, Mrs. Bishop's and Queen Emma's *kāhili* being among the first items to arrive in March.[71] A short time later, a writer for *The Friend* made a quick visit to the Museum: "A stolen glance into the building, the other day, revealed an interior of most rich and elaborate cabinet work, glass cases and tiled floors. Many important objects were in place, such as kahilis and carved work. Great quantities of curiosities were awaiting arrangement. Of course, there is a wonderful wealth and variety."[72]

51

Kāhili Room, for exhibition of Hawaiian birds, featherwork, mats, bark cloth, corals, etc. Photo attributed to W. T. Brigham, circa 1892.

Brigham's task of cataloging and arranging the collectons was hampered by lack of anything remotely resembling a laboratory, not to mention storage or suitable display facilities. "In the empty building there was a small closet under the stairs," he commented many years later, "but not a room for storage or preparing specimens. There were cases in the Kahili room but none in the larger room, now the Hawaiian Vestibule . . . When the Government museum was turned over to the infant museum the collections were piled on the floor of the Picture Gallery or stored in spare rooms in the school outhouses."[73]

Once Brigham began to move Bishop's collections into the Museum, it became painfully apparent that facilities were already inadequate for the expanded role the institution had assumed in the interval since the building had been designed. It was clear that improvements had to be made, and changes brought about by Brigham's insistence were not long in being announced (Brigham, 1916b, p. 122). Although ground would not be broken for the new wing until October,

First exhibits typical of the period. Hawaiian Vestibule looking beyond Entrance Hall into Kāhili Room.
Photo attributed to W. T. Brigham, circa 1892.

Picture Gallery, located above Hawaiian Vestibule, and beginnings of
Bishop Museum Library. Photo attributed to W. T. Brigham, circa 1892.

Rear view of Museum showing Polynesian Hall under construction,
future location of offices, laboratories, and two floors of exhibition galleries.
Photo attributed to W. T. Brigham, 1893.

1892,[74] plans for Polynesian Hall (completed in August, 1894) were revealed within two months after Brigham assumed office as curator. "We learn that the objects of Hawaiian antiquity and art, now in the progress of arrangement by Prof. Brigham, will more than fill the splendid new building," the *Daily Bulletin* reported on April 2, 1891. "Mr. Bishop has accordingly determined to proceed with the erection of a large addition, to be occupied with similar objects representing the other islands of Oceania. Negotiations are already in progress for extensive acquisitions by exchange and purchase from collections in Australia and New Zealand." One of the first of these new acquisitions materialized a month later, when the Museum purchased for $500 a collection of ethnographic specimens from German New Guinea assembled by a former resident of the area.

Though far from finished, installation of the first exhibits was well enough along to permit a formal opening on June 22 and 23, 1891, in connection with Kamehameha Schools' commencement celebrations. Queen Liliʻuokalani and her party signed the Museum's leatherbound register as the first official guests, just ahead of Henry Nanpei, a visiting chief from Ponape, Caroline Islands. The brief previews proved so popular that Brigham succumbed to demands and opened the Museum a few hours daily for the week beginning June 27, after which the doors were closed to all but special visitors until February to allow uninterrupted work on the collections.[75]

54

Polynesian Hall (rear) just after completion in 1894, partly visible behind Kāhili Room. Mr. Bishop paid for the new addition, which cost about $50,000. Photographer unknown.

A reporter attending commencement exercises recorded these impressions of the Museum on opening day:

> At the close, Principal W. B. Oleson, after thanking the audience for their kind attendance, extended an invitation to all to visit one of the classrooms (where the handicraft of the boys were exhibited) and the Bishop Museum. At the latter place, Prof. W. T. Brigham, curator, received the visitors and showed them around the halls in the lower story where relics of Hawaiian antiquities were kept in large show cases. Many aged Hawaiians recognized among the large collection idols which their ancestors reverenced with fear and awe. The god of Kamehameha I, and a god of rain attracted a large share of their attention.
>
> In the makai hall [Kāhili Room] is kept native mats and tapas, kahilis, the late Queen Emma's feather cloak, carried by Vancouver to England, and returned by the British Museum recently. This cloak is over one hundred years old, yet looks quite new. The workmanship is exceedingly fine. It requires perhaps several days to thoroughly inspect these rare remains of barbaric ages, and transient visitors can but form little impression of their value.[76]

The brief preview over, Brigham continued to arrange and classify the Museum's collection. By February, 1892, only one room was unfinished, and the Museum opened free to visitors one morning a week, usually Thursdays.[77] Brigham was also preparing a written catalog of the collections, partly for the convenience of visitors, but also for exchange to institutions abroad with   55

Polynesian Hall galleries shortly after opening to the public, December 19, 1894. Photo attributed to W. T. Brigham.

which he wished to establish formal contacts. The first part of the catalog was submitted to the trustees on June 17; they authorized its publication, as well as the Museum's closing at the end of the month so the curator could finish the catalog and proceed to field collecting and another trip to Australia and New Zealand.[78] By the end of the summer, Brigham had essentially finished with the *Preliminary Catalogue,* describing some 7,000 ethnographic and natural history specimens (Brigham, 1892-1893).[79] The trustees then decreed, on September 6, 1892, that until further notice the Museum would be open two days each week, Friday from 9:00 to 12:00, and Saturday from 2:00 to 5:00.[80]

Throughout the course of cataloging and arranging the exhibits, Brigham remained acutely aware of the unstable conditions under which the National Museum collection was in the custody of Bishop Museum. As a loan from a government sympathetic to the interests of the institution, there would be no problem, but with the unpredictable political situation confronting Hawai'i following the overthrow of Queen Lili'uokalani on January 17, 1893, he was well aware that this could easily change. In the event of annexation by the United States or some other foreign power, he feared the government collection might be confiscated and taken from the islands.

Brigham also had serious reservations about the overall quality of the government collection. While some of the specimens were useful for filling lacunae in the Museum's holdings, "many were decayed and insect eaten owing to neglect or ignorance of museum methods" (Brigham, 1916b, p. 122). Yet, with legal title still vested in the government, Brigham lacked freedom to exchange duplicate or secondary materials, the normal practice for upgrading museum collections everywhere. His concern is evident in an early report to the trustees: "The very unsatisfactory tenure by which we hold the collections of the former Government Museum, renders utterly useless a considerable number of duplicates which might and should be exchanged for valuable material."[81]

For the next few years, through petitions and correspondence to the various administrations ruling Hawai'i after the Monarchy's demise, Brigham tried with disappointing results to settle the question of title to the collections of the former Hawaiian National Museum. A blusterous and hastily written letter addressed to his old friend, "Hon. S. B. Dole, Minister of Foreign Affairs," on

Polynesian Hall accumulating natural history specimens, before extensive renovations in the 1950's. Bishop Museum photo, after 1917

June 7, 1893, shortly after declaration of the Provisional Government, reveals much about the mood then prevailing.

> I have only a newspaper report to go by, but that tells me that the Council voted to require insurance on the articles deposited by a former Government within this Museum. Allow me to protest against any such course. As a matter of law the present Government cannot so modify the existing agreement as to put any additional burden upon the present custodians of these articles. There was no insurance on these curiosities while in the Government Building exposed to fire all the time, and now that they are in a fire-proof building it seems less needful. With the exception of the feather cloaks, the entire collection is not worth, in my opinion, $500, much of it is utterly worthless to us as duplicates we cannot exchange, and I should advise the Museum Trustees to return the entire collection to the Government, rather than assume any additional burdens on it . . . I have twice petitioned the Government to give outright the contents of the old museum, but no notice has been taken of my request, so far as I have been informed. I must now request the Trustees to return the entire collection to the Government, so large a part of it being quite useless to us as we cannot exchange it.[82]

Seven years ensued before ownership of the Hawaiian National Museum collection was formally settled. Finally in the wake of annexation by the United States, a Joint Resolution passed by the Legislature of 1898 was signed on July 8 by S. B. Dole, President of the Republic of Hawai'i, authorizing the "transfer of ownership of all of the said articles heretofore loaned . . . for the purposes of the said Bernice Pauahi Bishop Museum, and without pecuniary consideration."[83]

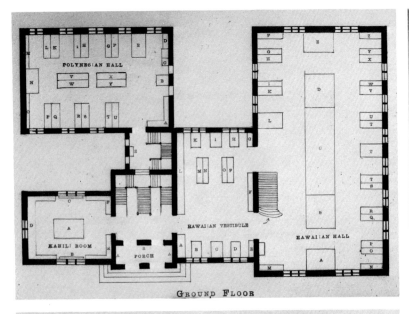

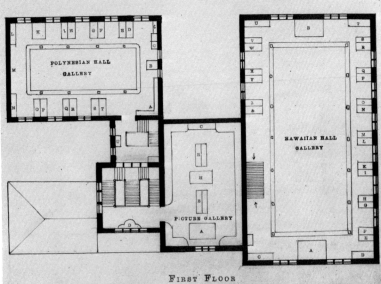

(Top and bottom) Bishop Museum exhibition halls,
with Hawaiian Hall annex to right, after 1900.

Hawaiian Hall interior under construction, 1899. Steel columns and
capitals were ornamented with Hawaiian plant and *kapa* (bark cloth) motifs
designed by Allen Hutchinson. (Compare with photo on page 64).
Photographer unknown.

EPILOGUE

Soon after much of Bishop's collection had been moved into the Museum from his Emma Street house, Brigham was himself the subject of another "transfer" of no little significance. The change occurred on March 23, 1891, when Bishop conveyed to the trustees of the Bishop Estate both the Museum building and its contents, which belonged to him, at the same time placing Brigham (whose salary he continued to pay) under the trustees' supervision.[84] In theory, this change placed the Museum on a separate but equal footing with The Kamehameha Schools, both of which continued to be administered by the same Board of Trustees.

Financially, this transfer led to the establishment of a separate Museum Trust in June, 1892. Setting aside the lands of Waipi'o, Hawai'i, proceeds from which were to be used for operation of the Museum, Bishop announced at the trustee meeting of June 17 that "after July, 1892, he would

Rear view of Museum showing Hawaiian Hall under construction, 1899, opposite Polynesian Hall (right). Designed by Ripley and Dickey, the building was erected by Arthur Harrison for approximately $62,000 and paid for by Mr. Bishop. The frame house originally built for Principal Oleson in 1886 had to be moved 100 feet to the left to accommodate the new annex. Photo attributed to W. T. Brigham.

Hawaiian Hall, completed in September, 1900, awaits installation of exhibit cases. Prefabricated from Hawaiian *koa* wood in Stillwater, Minnesota, and fitted with special locks and air seals, the ornate cabinetry eventually cost more than half as much as the building itself. Taro leaf and *kāhili* grillwork offest with the Hawaiian coat-of-arms was custom designed to enhance the hall. Photo attributed to W. T. Brigham.

William Alanson Bryan, Taxidermist and Curator of Ornithology, inspects sperm whale skeleton obtained from Ward's Natural Science Establishment before papier-mâché body is modeled over half the giant leviathan. The first exhibit in Hawaiian Hall, it may also be the first of its kind in the world. Photo attributed to W. T. Brigham, 1901.

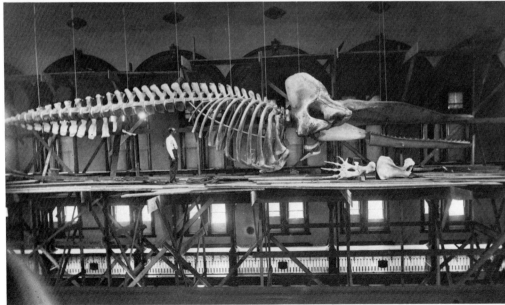

An old house frame from Kaua'i set up by Hawaiian house builders undergoes final thatching with *pili* grass. It is one of two traditional houses surviving in Hawai'i. The whale overhead now has its papier-mâché body. Photo attributed to W. T. Brigham, 1901.

no longer bear the expenses of the Museum. . . ."[84] With these preparations out of the way, Bishop contributed in March of the following year an additional $30,000 to the Museum endowment, the trustees agreeing "to safely invest said amount and to use the revenue only in procuring objects belonging to and illustrative of the life habits and customs of the aboriginal inhabitants of the Islands of the Pacific Ocean and of the natural history of said Islands and in the care, preservation and improvements of the said Museum" (Kent, 1965, p. 195). Additional gifts soon followed, and late in 1895 the Charles R. Bishop Trust was established to handle income from miscellaneous gifts and endowments to the Museum. This move also kept Museum funds separate from Bishop Estate accounts, which were devoted solely to maintenance of The Kamehameha Schools.

In 1896 a Deed of Trust was created at Bishop's request to facilitate administration of the Museum, formally separating it from the Bernice P. Bishop Estate. "The idea of making the 63

Hawaiian Hall about the time of dedication, November 24, 1903. Brigham visited leading museums around the world in 1896 (and again in 1912) to study latest developments in museum design and exhibition techniques. Photo attributed to W. T. Brigham.

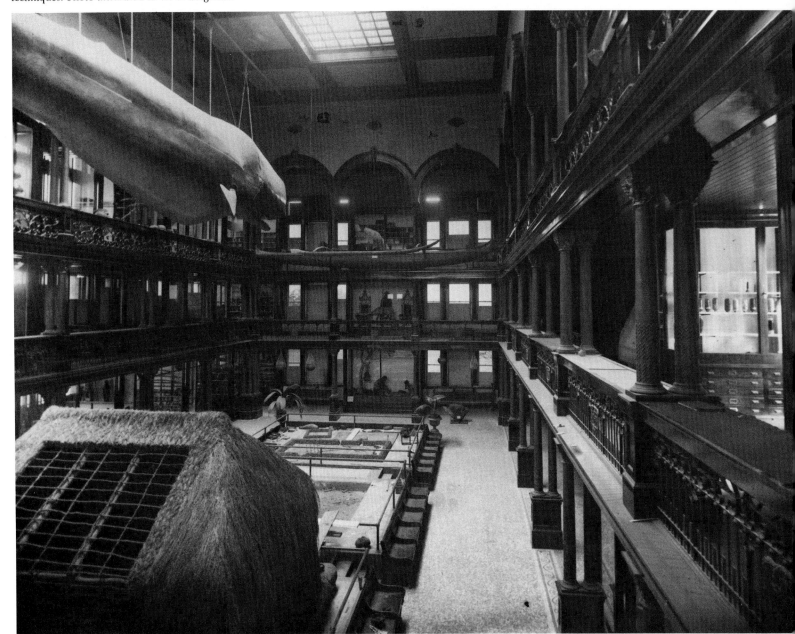

Scraping *olonā* fibers for cordage. This is one of six life-sized plaster figures commissioned for the new hall and modeled by Allen Hutchinson in 1896-97. Part of the set was later repeated for the Australian Museum, Sydney. Photo, L. E. Edgeworth, after 1913.

Museum a mere showplace for Polynesian antiquities has long since passed. . . . to confine the collection to things connected with the Islands of the Pacific would make the Museum unique and give it scientific value," Bishop admitted on directing Henry Holmes to work out details of the trust that February (Kent, 1965, pp. 196 - 197). Under the new Deed of Trust adopted later in the summer, administration of the Museum was placed in the hands of seven trustees, five of them Bishop Estate trustees (Bishop, Hyde, S. M. Damon, C. M. Cooke and J. O. Carter). At the first meeting of the new Trust October 28, 1896, Henry Holmes and S. B. Dole were voted in per Bishop's wish as the two additional members. At the second meeting, held December 2, Dole was elected Vice-President, though he continued to serve as chairman in the absence of President Bishop, who had moved to California in March, 1894. Never to return, Bishop resigned from both Trusts on October 13, 1897, and Dole became President of the Museum Trust (Kent, 1965, pp. 195-196).[85]

For Brigham, working under the new trustees proved trying in the extreme. Although conscientious, most of them had meager scientific backgrounds at best; their collective notions of museum management appeared at times to Brigham to be woefully limited, if not lacking altogether. Considering the numerous disagreements that were to develop over the next 20 years, Brigham would probably have stuck to one of his periodic threats to resign, had it not been for his

Hawaiians from Lunalilo Home, who have come to Bishop Museum "to sing into a phonograph"—an early project to preserve vanishing chants and songs on wax cylinders. Photo attributed to W. T. Brigham.

respect for Bishop, his friendship with Dole, and, despite numerous frustrations, his own belief in the institution.

Perhaps the most severe conflict arose in the summer of 1897, when Emma Nākuina, former curatrix of the Hawaiian National Museum, sent an angry letter of complaint to the trustees accusing Brigham of insulting her and a party of friends. Disturbed that an apparent misunderstanding had aroused her indignation, Brigham resigned as curator and threatened to return to the practice of law. Apparently relieved, the trustees accepted his resignation on July 9, placing Acland Wansey (who had returned after seven years' absence) in charge while a successor was sought. Immediately, Mrs. Nākuina applied for the position. Informed of these developments, Bishop, although mortified and indignant, in the end defended his temperamental but irreplaceable curator. "As you say, he may not be altogether truthful," Bishop pondered in a letter to trustee J. O. Carter, fully aware of Brigham's occasional tendency to exaggeration, "and I think it safe to say the same regarding her. She is a person of hot temper and strong prejudices, and seems to have had the mistaken idea that she is competent to fill the position held by Mr. Brigham."[86] Ultimately,

66

Bishop Museum staff circa 1901 assembled in unfinished Hawaiian Hall. From left: Allen M. Walcott, Assistant to the Director; Alvin Seale, Collector; John J. Greene, Printer; William T. Brigham, Director; William Alanson Bryan, Curator of Ornithology; John F. G. Stokes, Librarian and (later) Curator of Polynesian Ethnology. Bishop Museum photo.

Brigham was reinstated and promoted to Director, effective January 1, 1898, but the mutual enmity between Brigham and Nākuina persisted—with occasional flare-ups—until he became Director Emeritus in 1919.

Bouts of temperament aside, Brigham appreciated Bishop's confidence in his abilities, and all in all, the relationship proved remarkably productive over the years. For his part, Bishop gained from Brigham a broader understanding of museum concepts, which helped him sustain a paternalistic feeling toward the Museum and its work through the last days of his life. Bishop communicated part of this new philosophy to his curator the very day Brigham took up official connections with Bishop Museum: "The general indifference about preserving in the Country a good collection of native objects is remarkable. Neither native or foreigners seem to appreciate it at all. Is it not wise to let the natives know, through the papers published in their language, what is being done or attempted, and that old and rare things are wanted, partly for the sake of rising and future generations?"[87]

67

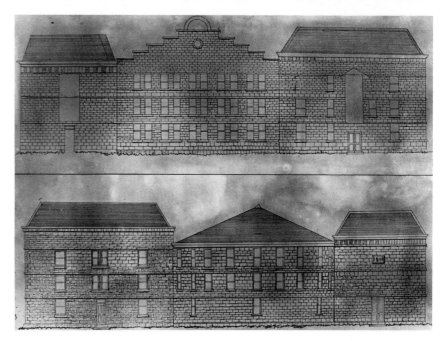

Front and rear elevations of proposed new laboratory, library, and exhibition hall, prepared under Brigham's direction in 1906 but never constructed, partly because of Bishop's losses in the great San Francisco earthquake and fire of April 18, 1906.

Sample floor plan from drawings for the proposed addition, which would have completed the central Museum complex in grand style.

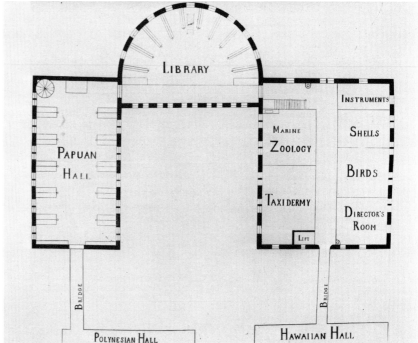

Bishop Museum Library, Hawaiian Hall third floor, before moving to new quarters in Pākī Hall in 1915. Taro and breadfruit leaf capitals were designed by Allen Hutchinson, who also sculpted the busts seen here of Mr. and Mrs. Bishop. Hutchinson based the keystone arch figures on a wooden image of Kālaipāhoa, the poison god (atop arch at left), after it was determined that ancient taboos would not be violated. Photo attributed to W. T. Brigham.

In a tribute written on Bishop's death, June 7, 1915, Brigham in a way summed up his own contribution to the relationship by recounting how he had been asked to arrange the collections in the new building.

> This I agreed to do that I might thus show my respect and affection for the memory of my friend [Mrs. Bishop]. This is not the place to detail the growth of this small beginning; wing after wing has been added, but at the time of Mr. Bishop's death the original plan was incomplete, and the fine building that had grown at the original giver's expense was not large enough for a proper scientific arrangement of its present contents, leaving out of view the probable future increase. The institution had ceased to be a mere curiosity shop, and had become well known all over the museum world by its publications which perhaps received more attention than they deserved coming from tiny isles in the midst of the great ocean, and made known the name of the founder and those of his trustees to all the principal libraries and museums in the civilized world; it was a working museum, and instead of amusing or instructing a few children of the Schools, it was attracting more than 1,500 visitors a month, and, better still, *students* from other parts of the world to its unrivalled Hawaiian collections (Brigham, 1916a, pp. 70 - 71).

69

Bishop Museum, circa 1915. Photographer unknown.

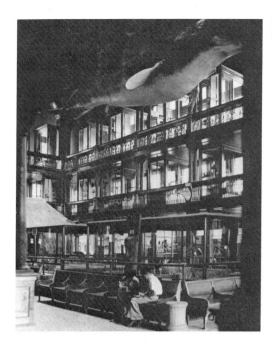

Hawaiian Hall, circa 1930's. Photo, Pan-Pacific Press Bureau.

Brigham himself was restrained in his comments about the defunct Hawaiian National Museum, notwithstanding his intimate acquaintance with many of its defects. Yet, on speaking at the dedication of Bishop Museum's Hawaiian Hall annex on November 24, 1903, he furnished what might aptly be termed an appropriate, if unwitting, epitaph to the Hawaiian National Museum—as well as a precept applicable to the future of museums the world over.

> This Museum is no longer merely an exhibition to amuse an idle hour, but it is, or should be when perfected, a means of collecting, preserving and studying the history of life in the Pacific . . . The amusement of the people, or even their instruction, is not the chief object of a museum such as this, but we have carefully collected all these things and clustered about them all the facts we can obtain and then we correlate these facts with others collected by workers in the same field until at last we may wrest from the unknown the secrets which today puzzle the wisest scientists . . .
>
> That is why a museum like this is never completed, indeed is never finally arranged. If it ceases to grow it dies, and its remains should be scattered to the four winds, that is, to enrich other living museums (Brigham, 1904. pp. 146 - 147).

71

Brigham relaxing in his garden. Photographer unknown.

Snapshot of Bishop at home in California. Until the end of his days he maintained a lasting interest in the museum founded in his wife's memory. Photographer unknown.

NOTES

1 Laws of His Majesty Kamehameha V, King of the Hawaiian Islands, Passed by the Legislative Assembly at Its Session, 1872. Ch. XXXIII, pp. 30 - 31.

2 Information on the Hawaiian National Museum contained herein is from an MS in preparation by the present author. Original documents are scattered in the Archives of Hawaii, mostly in the records of the Bureau of Public Instruction and the Foreign Office. See also Rose, 1977.

3 Bishop to Brigham, October 27, 1894. Manuscript Collection, Bishop Museum Library.

4 Quoted in *Daily Pacific Commercial Advertiser,* May 19, 1885.

5 *Daily Pacific Commercial Advertiser,* May 19, 1885.

6 *Saturday Press,* August 1, 1885.

7 Trustees' Minutes, Queen's Hospital, September 15, 1886; cited in Kent, 1965, p. 190.

8 *Daily Herald,* September 16, 1886.

9 The other three named to the Trust were Charles Montague Cooke, Samuel M. Damon, and William Oliver Smith, who later resigned and was replaced by Joseph O. Carter in October, 1886.

10 *Daily Bulletin,* April 7, 1886; *Daily Pacific Commercial Advertiser,* April 8, 1886.

11 *Daily Herald,* September 23, 1886; *Daily Bulletin,* October 18, 1886.

12 Hyde to Alden, November 6, 1886; cited in Kent, 1973, p. 169; Bishop to Brigham, July 8, 1895, Manuscript Collection, Bishop Museum Library. The two-story, wooden building, later and most inappropriately named Brigham House, was razed in February, 1979, to make way for the Atherton Hālau.

13 *Daily Pacific Commercial Advertiser,* January 12, 1887.

14 *Daily Bulletin,* November 3, 1887; Kent, 1973, p. 169.

15 *Daily Pacific Commercial Advertiser,* December 20, 1894.

16 Minutes of Meetings of Trustees, Bernice Pauahi Bishop Estate, October 21, 1887, excerpted in Minutes of Trustees of Bishop Museum, Director's Office, Bishop Museum.

17 *Daily Pacific Commercial Advertiser,* June 21, 1888.

18 *The Friend,* July, 1888.

19 *Daily Bulletin,* June 26, 1889.

20 *The Friend,* January, 1890.

21 *Daily Bulletin,* April 18, 1890.

22 Brigham to Wm. B. Lymer, December 30, 1916, Manuscript Collection, Bishop Museum Library.

[23] Brigham to Bishop, July 6, 1890. Manuscript Collection, Bishop Museum Library.

[24] Brigham to President and Council of the Boston Society of Natural History, January 21, 1864, Archives of the Boston Museum of Science.

[25] Brigham to John C. Merriman, May, 1923, Manuscript Collection, Bishop Museum Library.

[26] *Honolulu Advertiser,* February 17, 1926.

[27] Nordhoff to Brigham, December 1, 1873, Manuscript Collection, Bishop Museum Library; the autographed copy of Nordhoff's book is in Bishop Museum Library.

[28] Brigham to Dole, February 27, 1869, S. B. Dole Collection, Hawaiian Mission Children's Society.

[29] Brigham to Dole, February 10, 1867, Dole Collection, Hawaiian Mission Children's Society; Brigham to Herbert E. Gregory, July 10, 1922, Archives of Bishop Museum, Registrar's Office.

[30] Brigham to Dole, August 18, 1868, S. B. Dole Collection, Hawaiian Mission Children's Society.

[31] *Hawaiian Club Papers,* edited by a Committee of the Club. Boston: Kingman, 1868. p. 1.

[32] *The Friend,* May, 1874.

[33] Brigham to Dole, August 17, 1874, S. B. Dole Collection, Hawaiian Mission Children's Society.

[34] Brigham to Dole, April 15, 1880, S. B. Dole Collection, Hawaiian Mission Children's Society.

[35] *Hawaiian Gazette,* May 10 and July 28, 1880; December 7, 1881. Brigham was an accomplished photographer, having worked previously in Hawai'i in 1880 and in Central America between 1883 and 1886. Lecturing on the subject at various times, he read a paper on "The Dawn of Photography" before the annual meeting of the Boston Society of Amateur Photographers on February 5, 1883, which was published by the society.

[36] *Daily Bulletin,* March 17, 1887.

[37] A copy exists in Bishop Museum Library.

[38] Furneaux to Brigham, May 31, 1887, Manuscript Collection, Bishop Museum Library; Brigham to Dole, February 22, 1887, and June 21, 1887, S. B. Dole Collection, Hawaiian Mission Children's Society.

[39] Brigham to Dole, February 27, 1888, S. B. Dole Collection, Hawaiian Mission Children's Society.

[40] Brigham to Bishop, May 29, 1890, Manuscript Collection, Bishop Museum Library.

[41] Elsewhere Brigham (1916a, p. 70) also refers to correspondence with C. M. Hyde concerning the museum, but it has not come to light.

[42] Report of the Minister of Foreign Affairs to the Legislature of 1888, p. 7.

[43] Cabinet Council Minute Book, February 23, 1888, Archives of Hawaii.

[44] *Daily Bulletin,* March 13, 1886.

45 Brigham to Dole, May 19, 1888, Manuscript Collection, Bishop Museum Library.

46 Brigham to Dole, August 11, 1888, S. B. Dole Collection, Hawaiian Mission Children's Society.

47 *Hawaiian Gazette,* September 6 and 24, and October 2, 1888; *Daily Pacific Commercial Advertiser,* September 19, 21, 26, 27, and 28, 1888; *Daily Bulletin,* September 26 and 28, and October 2, 1888; *The Friend,* October, 1888.

48 Bishop to Brigham, December 13, 1888, Manuscript Collection, Bishop Museum Library.

49 Wansey to J. F. G. Stokes, August 1, 1920, Archives of Bishop Museum, Registrar's Office.

50 Cabinet Council Minute Book, February 25, 1889, Archives of Hawaii.

51 Mist to Brigham, February 27, 1889, Foreign Office Internal Letters, Vol. 69, p. 66; Foreign Office Diary, March 2, 1889, Archives of Hawaii.

52 List of Books to W. T. Brigham, February 25, 1889, Foreign Office Internal Letters, Vol. 69, pp. 62-63 (original copy in Private Collection M-418); Foreign Office Diary, March 13, 1889, Archives of Hawaii.

53 Wright to Mr. Sala, London, May 14, 1889, Foreign Office Letterbook 68; Brigham to Austin, May 9, FO & Ex Misc. Local; Archives of Hawaii.

54 Wansey to J. F. G. Stokes, August 1, 1920, Archives of Bishop Museum, Registrar's Office.

55 Accession Records, J. S. Emerson Collection, 1889.06, Bishop Museum.

56 Accession Records, American Board of Commissioners for Foreign Missions Collection, 1895.01, Bishop Museum.

57 Accession Records, J. S. Emerson Collection, 1889.06, Bishop Museum.

58 Receipt signed by G. Dole, May 27, 1889, FO & Ex Misc. Local; Foreign Office Diary, May 28, 1889, Archives of Hawaii; *Daily Bulletin,* September 28, 1889; *Daily Pacific Commercial Advertiser,* September 28, 1889; *Hawaiian Gazette,* October 1, 1889.

59 Brigham to Bishop, May 24, 1890, Manuscript Collection, Bishop Museum Library.

60 *Daily Bulletin,* July 7 and August 13, 1890.

61 Brigham to Bishop, July 6, 1890, Manuscript Collection, Bishop Museum Library.

62 Bishop to Brigham, August 18, 1890, Manuscript Collection, Bishop Museum Library.

63 Report of the Minister of Foreign Affairs to the Legislature of 1890, pp. 16-17.

64 Wansey to J. F. G. Stokes, August 1, 1920, Archives of Bishop Museum, Registrar's Office.

65 *Daily Pacific Commercial Advertiser,* June 9, 1888.

66 *Daily Bulletin,* February 18, 1890; see also *Daily Pacific Commercial Advertiser,* February 19, 1889 and *Hawaiian Gazette,* February 26, 1889.

[67] Foreign Office Diary, August 19 and October 29, 1890, Archives of Hawaii.

[68] Foreign Office Diary, October 20, 1890, Archives of Hawaii.

[69] Bishop to Brigham, February 17, 1891, Manuscript Collection, Bishop Museum Library.

[70] Brigham to Spencer, September 23, 1891, FO & Ex Misc. Local; Foreign Office Diary, November 23, 1891, Archives of Hawaii; Trustees' Minutes, November 20, 1891, Director's Office, Bishop Museum.

[71] *Handicraft,* March, 1891.

[72] *The Friend,* May, 1891.

[73] Brigham to Herbert E. Gregory, July 10, 1922, Archives of Bishop Museum, Registrar's Office.

[74] *Handicraft,* October, 1892.

[75] *Daily Bulletin,* June 22 and 27, 1891; *The Friend,* July 1891.

[76] *Daily Pacific Commercial Advertiser,* June 24, 1891.

[77] Trustees' Minutes, February 22, 1892, Director's Office, Bishop Museum; *Handicraft,* February and March, 1892.

[78] Trustees' Minutes, June 17, 1892, Director's Office, Bishop Museum.

[79] Trustees' Minutes, October 3, 1892, March 25 and May 19, 1893, Director's Office, Bishop Museum.

[80] Trustees to Brigham, September 6, 1892, Manuscript Collection, Bishop Museum Library.

[81] Report of the Bernice Pauahi Bishop Museum for 1894, by Wm. T. Brigham, Curator, Archives of Bishop Museum, Registrar's Office.

[82] Brigham to Dole, June 7, 1893, FO & Ex, President and Ministry of the Foreign Office, Archives of Hawaii. There were no feather cloaks or capes in the National Museum, properly speaking; the statement refers to featherwork transferred from 'Iolani Palace to Bishop Museum in 1893. Incidentally, the government collection was insured for $500 when deposited in Bishop Museum.

[83] Laws of the Republic of Hawaii Passed by the Legislature in Its Session, 1898, pp. 189-190.

[84] Trustees' Minutes, May 1, 1891. Director's Office, Bishop Museum.

[85] Unfortunately, inclusion of members of the Bishop Estate Trust on the Museum Trust proved to have been short-sighted; the resultant conflict of interest plagued the Museum until 1975, when the board of governance was finally changed.

[86] Bishop to Carter, July 6, 1897, Manuscript Collection, Bishop Museum Library.

[87] Bishop to Brigham, February 17, 1891, Manuscript Collection, Bishop Museum Library.

REFERENCES CITED

Alexander, Mary Charlotte, and Charlotte Peabody Dodge
  1941. *Punahou: 1841-1851.* Berkeley: Univ. California Press.

Barrot, Théodore-Adolphe
  1978. *Unless Haste is Made.* Kailua: Press Pacifica.

Bishop, Brenda
  1964-1965. The Bright Light of Knowledge. *Conch Shell* 2(1): 4-9; 2(2): 16-21; 2(3): 28-36; 2(4): 40-45; 3(1): 4-8.

Brigham, W. I. Tyler
  1907. *The History of the Brigham Family.* New York: Grafton Press.

Brigham, William T.
  1887. *Guatemala: The Land of the Quetzal, A Sketch.* New York: Scribner.
  1892-1893. *A Preliminary Catalogue of the Bernice Pauahi Bishop Museum of Polynesian Ethnology and Natural History,* Pts.
      1-4. Honolulu: Press Publishing Co.
  1904. Director's Report for 1903. *B.P. Bishop Mus. Occasional Pap.* 2(2): 143-170.
  1916a. Charles Reed Bishop: 1822-1915. *Hawaiian Annual.* pp. 63-71.
  1916b. Director's Report for 1915. *B.P. Bishop Mus. Occasional Pap.* 6(3): 119-190.

Damon, Ethel M.
  1957. *Sanford Ballard Dole and His Hawaii.* Palo Alto: Pacific Books.

Kay, E. Alison [Editor]
  1968. The Sandwich Islands. From Richard Brinsley Hinds' Journal of the Voyage of the "Sulphur."
      Hawaiian J. History 2: 102-135.

Kent, Harold Winfield
  1965. *Charles Reed Bishop: Man of Hawaii.* Palo Alto: Pacific Books.
  1973. *Dr. Hyde and Mr. Stevenson.* Rutland and Tokyo: Tuttle.

Martin, Roy S., and Robert Ramsay
  1960. *Hawaiian Tramways.* San Marino, California: Golden West Books.

Rose, Roger G.
  1977. A Centennial of Hawaiian Museums. *Hawaii Foundation for History and the Humanities, Summer Periodical.*

Schmitt, Robert C.
  1978. Some Firsts in Island Leisure. *Hawaiian J. History* 12: 99-119.